SYLVESTER

LECTURES ON THE

SCIENCE OF HUMAN LIFE

CONDENSED FOR THE ADVANTAGE OF THE GENERAL READER.

BY

T. BAKER, ESQ.,

OF THE INNER TEMPLE, BARRISTER-AT-LAW; SECRETARY TO THE ROYAL COMMISSION ON THE
SANITARY STATE OF THE ARMY IN INDIA (1859-63);
AUTHOR OF "THE LAWS RELATING TO PUBLIC HEALTH," "BURIALS," ETC

WITH COPIOUS INDEX,

COMPILED FOR THE SEVENTH EDITION OF THE COMPLETE WORK, BUT NOT APPEARING IN THE
AMERICAN EDITIONS.

"Know Thyself."

MANCHESTER: JOHN HEYWOOD, 141 AND 143, DEANSGATE;
THE VEGETARIAN SOCIETY'S DEPÔT, 91, OXFORD STREET.
LONDON:
JOHN HEYWOOD, 18, PATERNOSTER SQUARE; F. PITMAN, 20, PATERNOSTER ROW.

151. q. 97.

EDITOR'S PREFACE.

THE plan adopted in the following abridgment has been to alter nothing except by excision. There are no additions, and no salient point connected with the main subject—Human Physiology—has been omitted.

Sylvester Graham was a logician and a poet, as well as a scientific physiologist. His power of reasoning led him to work out each proposition in every variety of form, often being at great pains to state the argument of those who had upheld a different theory, in order to disprove their illusions; whilst his love for the beautiful was productive of abundant rhetorical ornament. Add to this that he wrote for oral delivery in separate lectures, and we have more than sufficient to account for a highly redundant style, including those diffuse repetitions which, so far from making a work more clear, render it both tiresome and obscure to the general reader.

The student is, nevertheless, strongly recommended to peruse these lectures in their original form. Comparison with this abridgment on any point will be easy, because the numbering of each paragraph used has been maintained; and an index, presumably prepared by, or at the instance of, the late Mr. George Dornbusch, is added to this volume entire, and will, therefore, serve as a key to the complete work at the same time. No index was made by the author, so that reference was extremely difficult.

These lectures, first published in 1839, were the result of many years intense devotion to the investigation of human physiology; and perhaps no book exists in any language more important in its aim, or more worthy of analytical exposition, than these "Lectures on the Science of Human Life."

Kingscote, Wokingham, January, 1876.   T. B.

MEMOIR.

THE author's father, the Rev. John Graham, graduate of Oxford (a collateral of the ducal house of Montrose), emigrated to Boston, U.S., in 1718. He must have been upwards of ninety years old when his seventeenth child, Sylvester, was born at Suffield, Connecticut, in 1794. Naturally delicate and sickly, the boy's life was preserved only by being early allowed to run wild among farmers. At twelve he went to school. He was handsome, clever, and imaginative. " I had heard of noble deeds, and longed to follow to the field of fame." Ill health soon obliged his return to the country, and at sixteen symptoms of consumption appeared. Various occupations were tried, amongst which his education was picked up, until the time, when about twenty years of age, he commenced as a teacher of youth, proving highly successful with his pupils. Again ill health obliged the abandonment of this pursuit.

In 1823 he resolved to study for the ministry at Amherst, and excelled as an elocutionist. He married in 1826, and soon after took up the temperance cause, which led him, amid frequent nervous attacks, to study with all his natural ardour, anatomy and physiology, becoming conspicuous in 1832 in his efforts to teach persons how to avoid the cholera which raged at that time. To the adoption of simple habits he ascribed his ability to carry his enfeebled constitution through the arduous labours he imposed on himself as a lecturer for the public good, but under which he at length broke down. He died on the 6th September, 1851, at Northampton, Massachusetts, aged fifty-eight.—*See Life and Character of Sylvester Graham, by F. Towgood.*

CONTENTS.

ABRIDGMENT OF

LECTURES ON THE SCIENCE OF HUMAN LIFE

BY

SYLVESTER GRAHAM.

I.

1. MAN is the soul of the world—the intellectual and moral sensorium of nature. He is not, indeed, the creating *cause* of things, nor is he the efficient *energy* by which the various operations of nature are carried on. Yet, but for man, to what great intellectual and moral end would all things exist ?

3. He opens his percipient faculties on the surrounding world, and all things become to him the great alphabet of knowledge, until he learns to arrange these elements into systems, and elaborates from them the principles of science !

5. All things in nature are endowed by him with their peculiar genii, and become the talismanic keys which awaken appropriate tones within his breast.

8. Whatever, therefore, may be the interest connected with material things, man is the centre of that interest.

9. An attempt to study living man, without a just regard to his peculiar nature, and the various influences which act upon him, would necessarily result in error.

10. If we would know the true philosophy of the human mind, it is not enough that we study man's intellectual faculties ; but we must ascertain how far the mind is connected with the body, and on what depends those conditions of the body which affect the mind.

11. So, likewise, if we would understand the science of physiology, we must take into view the whole nature of man. He who treats of the functions of the human organs without fully considering the modifying influences of the mind, may form a theory which will have its day of popular acceptance, but fortunate will it be if it does not prove to possess sufficient errors to sink it into disrepute.

12. There is probably no subject concerning which more extensive error prevails than in regard to life, health, and disease. In relation to almost everything else mankind are willing to acknowledge that there are fixed laws and an established order.

13. If we assert that God has constructed the planetary system upon fixed principles, or that, in the creation of our globe, he has established unchanging

laws, our affirmation will be promptly acceded to. Yet, if we turn to the higher order of God's works, and affirm that human life and health are governed by laws as precise, mankind will, almost universally, deny the affirmation, and contend that health and disease are matters of uncertainty, governed by no laws, and subject only to the arbitrary control of God, the blind necessity of fate, or contingency of accident. They do not believe that there are any fixed laws of life by which man can preserve health, and prolong his existence.

15. In the same circumstances, they affirm, one enjoys health, and another is frequently diseased ; one dies early, and another reaches an advanced period of life ; while people of very different habits experience the same uncertainties ; and in all circumstances the vigorous often die suddenly in the very prime of life, while the feeble drag out a protracted existence. Survey the earth, and we find the inhabitants of one portion feeding on putrescent carcases, others on vermin, others on a mixture of animal and vegetable substance, others on vegetables exclusively, and others allaying their hunger with unctuous earths ; some indulging freely in tobacco, others in opium, others in arrack, others in some of the numerous forms of alcohol ; and yet, with these differences we find, it is said, among all the different tribes of the human family about an equal share of health and disease, premature death and extended life.

16. Thus, we are told, it is demonstrated by experience that human life, health, and disease are matters either of fatality or contingency ; in regard to them, there is no fixed philosophical relation between cause and effect ; and therefore, the life, health, disease, and diet of man cannot be governed by fixed laws, nor made matters of systematic science.

17. This reasoning, at first, appears conclusive ; but, when examined, it proves fallacious : the more deeply we push our investigations, the more are we convinced that human life and health are matters of nearly exact science. Human physiology is the most important science ; and, to the perfect under standing of it, a knowledge of all other sciences is requisite.

18. In the state of nature the wants of man are few and simple.

19. The *rational powers* are little employed in investigating the adaptation of his diet to the laws of organic vitality. He feels his wants, is prompted to satisfy them ; and is governed by those instinctive powers of smell and taste, which enable him to discriminate between esculent and poisonous substances. And, if reasoning powers of a higher order are employed, it is in devising the means by which his supplies are procured, rather than in ascertaining the fitness of those supplies to the wants of his nature.

20. As man becomes removed from the state of nature by artificial habits, he finds it *convenient* to possess those utensils with which he prepares his food and fits his clothing for his body. No sooner are these things considered *necessary*, than the supply becomes of nearly as much importance as food, drink, and clothing ; and in the development of this state the several arts and sciences are matured.

22. In the progress of these arts, one want has created another, and caused a continual demand for the closest application of the mental powers to the investigation of the physical, mechanical, and chemical properties of things,

and with reference to forces, motions, numbers, quantities, time, distance, etc., etc., till mathematics, astronomy, chemistry, etc., have been developed.

23. But in this general progress, there is little to lead the mind to study life, or examine the habits of civil life with reference to health and disease.

25. It is true that disease multiplies in proportion as man removes from a state of nature and becomes an artificial being, and this leads to the study of the healing art.

26. Disease always precedes the physician; and the sick are only concerned to know how they can obtain relief from their sufferings. The question with them is not how they came by their sickness, or by what violations of the laws of life, but by what remedies they can restore health.

28. It follows that individuals become devoted to the study of remedies; and thus physicians originate. But everything is done with a view to *cure* the disease, without any regard to its cause; and the disease is considered as the infliction of some supernatural being; therefore, in the progress of the healing art thus far, not a step is taken towards investigating the laws of health and the philosophy of disease.

29. Nor, after medicine had received a more systematic form did it lead to those researches which were most essential to its success; but, like religion, it became blended with superstitions and absurdities. Hence, the history of medicine, with very limited exceptions, is a tissue of ignorance and error, and only serves to demonstrate the absence of that knowledge upon which alone an enlightened system of medicine can be founded; and to show to what extent a noble art can be perverted from its capabilities of good to almost unmixed evil, by the ignorance, superstition, and cupidity of man.

31. In modern times, anatomy and surgery have been carried nearly to perfection, and great attainments have been made in physiology. The science of human life has been studied with interest and success; but this has been confined to the few; while, even in our day, and in the medical profession itself, the general tendency is adverse to the diffusion of scientific knowledge.

32. Intent as all men are on enjoyment, they are little inclined to practise self-denial for the sake of a good, in any possible degree contingent. Hence, so long as mankind are favoured with a moderate degree of health, they rush into the excitement of pleasure. While they possess health, they will not believe that they are in danger of losing it; or if they are, nothing in their habits can have any effect in destroying or preserving it: nor can they be convinced of the delusion that, if they enjoy health, they have within themselves the demonstration that their habits are conformable to the laws of health. They will not, therefore, consent to be benefited, contrarily to what they regard as necessary to their enjoyment, by the experience or learning of others.

33. The consequence is that mankind prodigally waste the resources, as if the energies of life were inexhaustible; and when they have brought on disease which destroys their comforts, they fly to the physician, not to learn by what violation of the laws of life they have drawn the evil upon themselves, and by what means they can avoid the same; but, considering themselves visited with afflictions which they have in no manner been concerned in causing, they require the physician's remedies, by which their sufferings

may be alleviated. In doing this, the more the practice of the physician conforms to the appetites of the patient, the greater is his popularity, and the more generously is he rewarded.

34. Everything, therefore, in society tends to confine the practising physician to the department of therapeutics, and make him a mere curer of disease ; and the consequence is, that the medical fraternity have little inducement to apply themselves to the study of the science of life, while, almost everything by which men can be corrupted is presented to induce them to become the mere panders of human ignorance and depravity ; and if they do not sink to the vilest empiricism, it is owing to their own moral sensibility, rather than to the encouragement they receive to pursue an elevated scientific professional career.

35. Thus the natural and acquired habits of man concur to divert his attention from the study of human life ; and hence he is left to *feel* his way to, or gather from, what he calls *experience*, all the conclusions which he embraces.

36. This source of knowledge is as fallacious as it is specious ; and the more deeply mankind are betrayed by it, the more blinded do they become to its treachery, and confidently contend for its validity.

37. Everyone *knows*, from his own *feelings* and *experience*, what kind of constitution he has, and what disagrees with it, and what agrees with his stomach. If a lady has the headache, she knows her own feelings ; and if she drinks a strong cup of tea, and the pain leaves her head, nobody ought to be guilty of so gross an insult to her understanding as to attempt to convince her that tea is a poison, and that her use of it is a principal cause of her headache. She always feels better after drinking tea ; and, from experience, she knows that there is no better remedy, for she has been subject to headache twenty years, and the violence has increased till she is obliged to give up all pleasures, and take to her bed whenever she has a turn ; and she has found that tea is "the sovereignest remedy in the world" for headache ! Who can reason against such facts ? or advance a theory which contradicts universal experience ? The enterprise is arduous, and cheered by no encouraging prospect.

38. I do not wish to convince my fellow-creatures that they have no *feelings*, but to convince them that feelings by no means teach causes nor principles. I concede to the lady that she knows how her headache feels ; and that it is relieved by a cup of tea. But does she know the remote or immediate cause of her headache ? Does she know the qualities of the tea in relation to the vital and functional powers of her system, and the ultimate effects of the tea ? How it produces the pleasurable feelings, how it removes the pain ? And whether the effects of the tea, by which the paroxysms are relieved, are not the principal source of her headache ? If not, what are her feeling and experience worth ? I answer, not a farthing. Nay, they are worse than nothing — mere delusions ! And such is the experience of mankind. I acknowledge that they *feel* ; but do they know physiologically *how* or *why* they feel ? I acknowledge that, by virtue of a vigorous constitution, many may live to old age, in ordinary health, in spite of habitual violations of the laws of life. But does this constitute an experience which proves the correctness of their habits ? Most evidently it does not.

39. It has been observed "that men in their inductive reasonings deceive themselves continually, and think that they are reasoning from facts and experience, when they are only reasoning from a mixture of truth and false-hood. The only end answered by facts so incorrectly apprehended is that of making error more incorrigible. Nothing, indeed, is so hostile to the interests of truth as facts incorrectly observed." On no subject are men so liable to misapprehend facts, and mistake the relation between cause and effect, as on that of human life, health, and disease. Without profound physiological knowledge it is not possible to avoid self-deception. They mistake the *causes*, and misunderstand the pathological character of the feelings. Judging the qualities of things by the feelings they produce, without considering that baneful substances may be made the causes of pleasurable stimulation to depraved organs, they confound good and evil, their facts become falsehoods, their inductions erroneous, and their experience a tissue of error and absurdity, which serves only to mislead and betray.

40. Nothing is more certain, therefore, than that the only way by which mankind can attain to correct notions concerning human life is to study the subject as a science ; and this will lead them, as rational beings, over a most extensive field of investigation.

41. Could we seize upon vitality, and ascertain its essence, we might reason from its intrinsic powers with less help from other sciences than we now find requisite. But we know nothing of the essence of life, and can only know its peculiar properties by ascertaining the character of its manifestations in relation to the ordinary laws of inorganic matter.

42. We perceive, therefore, that the science of Human Nature is most comprehensive, as well as complicated and profound.

II.

Lecture II. (47—111) *is occupied in discussing the forms and properties of inorganic matter.*

III.

Lecture III. (112—138) *treats of the relation of organic matter to the inorganic world ; and of the powers peculiar to animal, as distinguished from vegetable bodies.*

139. The fondness of chemists to account for the results of vitality upon chemical principles has led them to retard science, by preventing that investi-gation of the vital forces which is necessary to a full ascertainment of the laws of life. No organic substance can be separated from the vital control, and subjected to experiment, without so altering the substance as to render it impossible for the chemist to affirm what is true of the processes of the living system. It is much more accurate for chemists to say what inorganic forms result from a chemical analysis of organic substances, than it is to state that organic substances are composed of such and such chemical elements. We have no right to assume that vital forces possess no higher energies than are exerted by chemical agents ; nor that their principles resemble those of inorganic chemistry. Vitality decomposes all those substances which chemists call elements ; and, in arranging its organic structures, its operations are

different from those of inorganic chemistry. It is hypothetical to assert that oxygen, carbon, hydrogen, azote, and other elements, as such, combine to form the various structures of the organic system. Nevertheless, it remains true that the differences between forms of matter consist in, and spring from, the laws which govern their component particles and *constitute the peculiar nature of each form.*

140. THE NATURE OF THINGS DEPENDS IN NO DEGREE ON THE MATTER OF WHICH THEY ARE FORMED, BUT ENTIRELY ON THE CONSTITUTIONAL LAWS OF ARRANGEMENT AND STRUCTURE, FROM WHICH THE PECULIAR PROPERTIES OF THINGS RESULT.

IV.

145. All solid bodies are formed from fluids. In the mineral kingdom, the structure of some solid masses indicates a previous state of fusion, while others indicate a state of aqueous fluidity. ·

146. In the vegetable kingdom, all solid substances are formed from the sap, which is little else than water, and is gradually changed into vegetable structure by the powers of the vegetable economy. In the animal kingdom, all the solid substances composing the body are formed from the watery fluid called chyle, which is elaborated from the food, converted into blood, and arranged into solids by the animal vitality.

147. When chyle, blood, bone, muscle, &c., have been elaborated by the vital economy, chemists subject them to analysis, and denominate the substances obtained the organic elements ; and, taking these results of the analysis of dead matter, account for the operations of the living economy on the principles of inorganic chemistry, and teach what elements combine to form the organic system. But most of their reasoning assumes that the decomposition of *dead* matter demonstrates the vital composition of *living* matter. But if chemical elements, as such, combine to form any one substance, why is it not possible for science to make any approach to vital processes ?

148. The human bone is composed of gelatin, phosphate of lime, &c., and these are formed by oxygen, hydrogen, carbon, azote, phosphorus, &c. But can philosophers compose bone? Or do they believe there is any power by which the bone can be composed except the vital power of the system? Whether phosphoric acid and lime, *as such*, enter into the vital composition of the bone it is not possible to prove; and science affords less evidence of the fact than it does that the economy by which bone is formed was originated by an intelligent Creator. Nor would it be easier for chemical physiologists to demonstrate that the gelatin in animal bodies is formed from the blood by a process which abstracts a portion of its carbon, *as such;* nor can it be proved that any chemical element, *as such*, passes through the vital operations, retaining its peculiar nature, or without foregoing the qualities it possessed as an inorganic substance.

149. All we know is—that, when substances are received into the organs of the system, they are converted into chyme, chyle, and blood, and from the blood into solids and fluids, possessing each its peculiar properties; the solids to form the organs of the system, and the fluids in such conditions as the vital domain requires.

150. To ascertain the properties and operations of the living body is the business of the physiologist. When the body is dead, the dissection of its organs is the business of the anatomist; and the analysis of the dead matter into elements is, appropriately and only, the business of the chemist.

151. Chemistry can tell us what forms of inorganic matter result from a chemical analysis of dead animal matter; but she cannot tell us what forms compose the living organ. She cannot inform us *à priori* whether mineral, vegetable, or animal substances are adapted to the alimentary wants of man; nor direct us in the selection of substances nourishing to the body. She can decompose the atmosphere, but cannot tell us which of its elements qualify it to support animal respiration. If in the stomach foreign acids be generated by inorganic affinities, chemistry can inform us what will neutralise those acids, but cannot tell us whether the alkalies will not do more mischief to the organ than the acids, or what is salutary to the vital weal. This we learn from the living body.

152. While, therefore, all honour is paid to chemistry, the sciences of physiology and therapeutics should be cautious how they invoke her aid. Chemistry can assist the physiologist in ascertaining the external relations of the body, but more she cannot do with that certainty which should inspire confidence.

153. The most simple form of matter composing the body is chyle, elaborated from the food in the alimentary canal. This is a thin, pearl-coloured fluid, and, by analysis, is almost wholly resolved into water. As it proceeds along the vitalising tubes, it becomes more albuminous and fibrinous; and with scarcely any difference whether the food be vegetable or animal; but in regard to vital properties differing considerably

154. When chyle enters the blood-vessels, it approaches nearly in character to blood, which is itself *apparently* a simple fluid, the constituents of which are albuminous; and of which four-fifths may be resolved to water.

155. From blood the vital economy elaborates all the substances composing the body, constructing the blood-vessels and the alimentary tube, with the organs of nutrition, and the limbs and organs of external relation.

156. The solid matter thus elaborated from blood may be reduced to three kinds of substances—the gelatinous, the fibrinous, and the albuminous; which, in physiology, are denominated the CELLULAR, the MUSCULAR, and the NERVOUS TISSUES.

157. Some physiologists assure us that the structure of the tissues is a delicate arrangement of minute globules, and that this is alike true of the cellular, muscular, and nervous tissues.

158. The gelatinous substance, in its forms of cellular tissue, membranes, tendons, ligaments, cartilages, &c., is the most simple of the animal solids, and the lowest in vital endowment. Its properties are cohesion, flexibility, elasticity; and, in some forms, extensibility.

159. The muscular tissue is of a higher order of vital endowment than the cellular. It possesses the vital properties of excitability and contractility under the action of stimulants.

160. It is impossible to say how far we can subject the tissues to analytical investigation without effecting an *essential* change in their nature; therefore

we cannot affirm that the substance on which we experiment is the same as when living. It is under this disadvantage we labour when we attempt to ascertain the character of the solids, or the results of vital action; and it is under this disadvantage that physiologists affirm that the nervous tissue is albumenous.

161. The nervous is the highest organised matter, and is endowed with wonderful properties. In descriptions of anatomy, it is said to consist of two substances. The one called cineritious, because the colour of ashes; sometimes cortical, because on the surface of the brain like the bark of a tree; and sometimes pulpy.

162. The other substance is called medullary, or the white substance, and more recently it has been called the fibrous substance. It is firmer than the pulpy, and is arranged in the form of minute fibres.

163. In every portion of the nervous apparatus the pulpy substance is associated with the fibrous; sometimes investing the surface, as in the brain, sometimes internally, as in the spinal marrow.

164. The powers of the nervous tissue are the nervous and sensorial. To the nervous belong the vital properties concerned in the functions of digestion, absorption, respiration, circulation, secretion, structure, and the production of heat. The transmission of impressions to the centre of perception, and of stimulus to the muscles, have also been classed among the nervous properties, but it is questionable whether the former function does not belong to the sensorial power.

165. To the sensorial power belong consciousness, sensation, the perception of impressions and affections, reflection, volition, and faculties called intellectual.

166. Sensibility is generally considered the fundamental sensorial power; yet the brain is destitute of the power of sensation. Sensibility, in the physiological signification, is the power of sensation in the tissue, and sensation is an affection of the tissue, of which the centre of perception is not only conscious, but refers it to some locality. Sensation, therefore, not only makes the mind conscious of a body, but of particular parts of the body. This is not true of the sensorial power. We may sink into reverie, and be only conscious of a mental existence. We *think*, and are conscious of our thoughts, but not of their machinery, still less do we refer them as sensations to the brain. At such times we are not conscious of a brain, nor anything of a corporeal nature. To say, therefore, that sensibility is the fundamental sensorial power, is to give the term a very broad signification, and to confound things between which there are important differences.

167. These three tissues—the cellular, muscular, and nervous—compose all the organs of the system, and each carries its peculiar properties, which become the principles of functional power in the organs.

168. The cellular tissue constitutes a framework to the body, giving shape to each organ, and entering so extensively into every part that if the other substances were abstracted, the cellular tissue would preserve the outlines and proportions of each.

169. Every bone partakes of this in a cellular arrangement, the interstices of which are filled with a fluid, separated from the blood, which becomes hard, and gives solidity to the texture. Some of the bones are united by this substance in the form of elastic cartilage, or fibro-cartilage, as the vertebræ of the back, the ribs to the sternum, &c. The articulating surfaces of the bones are also sheathed with cartilage. The joints are secured, and different bones bound together by another form of the same substance, called ligament. This last is expanded into a fibrous membrane, which surrounds every bone, also the cartilages, and forms sheaths for the tendons.

170. Besides this distribution to the bones, cartilages, and tendons, the cellular tissue forms sheaths for every muscle and every fibre, and composes the tendons and expansions which connect the muscles with the bones. Every fibre of the nervous system is also enveloped in a sheath of cellular tissue, and the brain and spinal marrow are wrapped in a texture of the same substance.

171. The different tissues are connected by the cellular; and each organ is enveloped, every internal surface lined, and the external surface covered, with membranes composed of this substance.

172. The contractility of the muscular tissue is the only element of motion in the body. All motion depends on this property of the muscle. Hence the muscular tissue is distributed where motion is required. The bones are incapable of motion within themselves, and consequently no muscular tissue enters into their texture. But they serve as levers, and the muscles of voluntary motion are attached to them in such a manner that the contraction of the muscles produces the motions required. The windpipe, meat-pipe, stomach, and intestines are also furnished with muscular tissue. The heart is muscular, and the diaphragm is composed of muscular tissue. Several other organs are supplied with this tissue. The arteries and veins are said to be destitute of it, and yet they possess the power of contractility.

173. The nerves preside over the vital economy, and are distributed to every part of the system, accompanying the blood-vessels, and associated with every muscular fibre.

174. The blood-vessels with their nerves are first produced, and these commence the structure of the alimentary tube with its organs, each according to its office, and the powers required for its special function. At first the organs are so many distinct formations, which become connected, and finally so associated as to form a single system. The spinal column and ribs form the trunk, which supports and protects them. The head, the upper and lower extremities, the organs of special sense, the skin, hair, and nails follow in their order.

175. For the protection of the organs, and other purposes, the body is divided by the diaphragm into two apartments. The upper is called the thorax, and the lower the abdomen. The thoracic cavity contains the lungs, heart, and meat-pipe. The abdominal cavity contains the liver, stomach, intestinal canal, pancreas, spleen, kidneys, &c.

176. The serous membrane lines both cavities, and is folded so as to envelope each organ and confine it to its proper place. Thus, in the chest, the serous membrane, here called the pleura, surrounds each lung, passes across, forming a double partition, called the mediastinum, and encloses each

B

lung in a sack on the right and left side of the thorax. The two sheets which form the partition are separated at the lower part to receive the heart. This organ is also surrounded by its own membrane, the pericardium. The serous membrane which lines the abdomen, and each organ of that cavity, has the name of peritoneum ; but its parts are designated by the organs invested. Thus, the part which embraces the intestinal tube, and holds its convolutions in their position, is the mesentery, mesocolon, &c.

177. In regard to the anatomy and physiology of the serous membrane there is difference of opinion. Some describe it as supplied with vessels containing a colourless fluid, performing the office of absorbents ; and this they consider proved by the fact that the serous membrane is capable of inflammation, as in pleurisy, peritonitis, &c. On the other hand, it is asserted that this membrane is destitute of vessels and nerves, and that fluids pass through it by infiltration. These deny that this membrane can be the seat of inflammation. They contend that the diseases have their seat in the tissue, and such is the thinness of the membrane that the inflamed aspect is seen through.

178. In a healthy state the serous membrane has no sensibility. Its surface is smooth, and lubricated by a fluid which is exhaled from its vessels, or passes through it from the subjacent vessels. By these means contiguous organs are enabled to move with ease, and adhesion is prevented. On the side of the membrane, next to the organs and the parts which it lines, it is covered with a spongy substance, which contains adipose matter. In fleshy people quantities of fat accumulate in this tissue (508).

179. The bones are of various forms and sizes. Some are hollow, and their cavities lined by a membrane, which contains an unctuous marrow. The number of bones in the body is two hundred and fifty-six ; of which fifty-six belong to the trunk, sixty-six to the head, sixty-eight to the upper, and sixty-six to the lower extremities.

180. Of the bones of the trunk, twenty-nine are employed in the construction of the spinal column ; twenty-four, called the true vertebræ, the other five the false vertebræ, or the sacrum and coccyx ; concerned also in the formation of the pelvis at the bottom of the trunk, the base on which the vertebral column rests. Of the true vertebræ, seven belong to the neck, twelve to the back, and five to the loins, distinguished by the terms cervical, dorsal, and lumbar vertebræ. These have somewhat the shape of a ring, with a rounded body in front, and several projections from behind ; one running directly back, called the spine, and two obliquely backward, with which the ribs form one of their points of attachment. The vertebræ are so constructed that they form a support to the body, and a canal for the spinal marrow. Between these bones is an elastic substance, which unites them, so as to give the column considerable flexibility, and secure all the supporting power of a solid bone. In the natural position the spinal column is curved ; and such is its elasticity, that an individual is sometimes an inch taller in the morning than at night.

181. Attached to each side of the twelve dorsal vertebræ are twelve ribs, which, with the breastbone, form the cavity of the chest. Most of the ribs have a double attachment behind, one to the vertebræ and one to the oblique projection. They droop so that their anterior extremities are lower than their

posterior. The upper seven, called true ribs, are united to the breastbone by cartilages. Of the remaining five, called false ribs, three are joined to the superior ribs by cartilages, and the two lowest, not connected, are called floating ribs.

182. Of the sixty-six bones which belong to the head, seven form the skull, which rests upon the spinal column, and receives the spinal marrow through a large opening. Four small bones constitute a part of the apparatus of each ear. The rest, beside the thirty-two teeth, form the jaws, cheeks, nose, palate, etc. There are in each jaw sixteen teeth, on each side two front, one corner, and five cheek teeth.

183. To the upper extremities belong, on each side, the shoulder-blade, collar-bone, long bone of the upper arm, two bones of the fore-arm, eight small bones of the wrist, five of the body of the hand, fourteen of the fingers and thumb, and the small appendage to the thumb-joint.

184. To the lower extremities, on each side, the hip-bone, long bone of the thigh, two bones of the lower leg, knee-pan, seven small bones of the ankle and heel, five bones of the instep, fourteen of the toes, and the small appendage to the great toe-joint.

185. Before the solidity of the bony structure is required, the place of the bones is occupied by cartilages the shape of the bones. As the time approaches when the functions of the system require protection, ossification commences, and continues till completed. As life advances the bones become hard, and in age, and some kinds of disease, very brittle. Where two bones are united, cartilages are interposed, and form the union ; in some cases firmly, as in the sutures of the skull, in other cases admitting flexion, as in the backbone and ribs. In all the movable joints the articulating surfaces are covered with highly-polished cartilages, continually lubricated by a fluid called synovia, by which the joints act with ease and little friction. Cartilage is employed separately in some of the cavities, as the larynx, wind-pipe, part of the nose, &c. The cartilages are, like the bones, surrounded by a membrane called the perichondrium. Anatomists differ in regard to the endowments of the cartilages. There is no reason to believe that they have any other nerves than those which belong to the vessels concerned in their nutrition (230) ; they have in health no sensibility (294), nor do their vessels contain any blood. In early life the cartilages are soft, they gradually become harder, and in age they lose their elasticity, become brittle, and some of them converted into bone, especially those of the fixed joints.

186. By this interposition of cartilaginous substance many advantages are gained. Besides the flexibility of the spinal column, the yielding of the ribs and other bones, friction is prevented in the joints, and elasticity is imparted to the frame, assisting in running, jumping, etc., and protecting us by breaking the force of blows, falls, &c.

187. The ligaments consist of strong fibres of cellular tissue. They connect the ends of bones and cartilages, secure the joints to prevent displacement, and allow necessary motion. Some are situated within the joint, like a central cord or pivot; some surround it like a hood, and contain the lubricating fluid ; some are in the form of bands at the side.

188. The ligaments bind the lower jaw to the temporal bones, the head to

the neck, extend the length of the backbone in powerful bands, bind the ribs to the vertebræ and to the breast-bone, and this to the collar-bone, and this to the shoulder-blade, and this to the bone of the upper arm, and this to the bones of the fore-arm at the elbow, and these to the wrist, and these to each other and to the hands, and these last to the fingers and thumb. In the same manner they bind the bones of the pelvis, and the hip-bones to the thigh, and this to the bones of the leg, and so on to the ankle, foot, and toes. Thus the osseous system is united, in the most admirable manner, so as to possess mobility and firmness. The ligaments, like the cartilages, are in health destitute of sensibility, are soft and yielding in early life, and become more inflexible in age.

189. The muscles constitute a considerable part of the body. They seem to consist of a confused mass of flesh adhering to the bones ; but the inquirer finds every part of the muscular system arranged in the most regular manner. On divesting the body of its skin, masses are seen running in various directions, some broad and thin, some narrow and thicker, some more rounded ; some of uniform size, some large in the middle and taper towards the extremities, and some spread out like a fan, long and short, running parallel with the bones, and obliquely or transversely. These are muscles, and each is surrounded by its sheath of gauzelike cellular tissue, the interstices of which are repositories of fat. The muscle is composed of parallel bundles, each of which is surrounded by a sheath. If these be opened, parallel fibres appear, also enveloped in sheaths, and each of these fibres is composed of minute filaments.

190. There is discrepancy among anatomists in regard to the muscular filament. But these points are of little importance. If we can ascertain the vital powers of the muscle, and know how they are affected, we possess all the knowledge in regard to the structure of the filament that can be of practical utility.

191. I have said (159) that the vital properties of muscle are—1st, susceptibility, or sensibility to stimulants ; 2nd, contractility, or the power to shorten under stimulation. These are generally regarded as a *single* property, and denominated muscular irritability : but they are different powers—the one to *receive* an impression, and the other to *act* under that impression.

192. The vital properties of the muscle are exhausted by action, and it is requisite that they should be replenished. This depends on the blood ; and it is necessary that the muscle be freely supplied. Accordingly, numerous arteries are distributed conveying to the muscular system blood to nourish its substance.

193. The nerves distributed to the muscles are of three kinds : 1. Those that accompany the blood-vessels. These are concerned in producing those changes in the blood necessary to the welfare of the muscle. 2. Those that convey the stimulus of the WILL. These divide and subdivide till too small to be detected, and act to stimulate the muscle. 3. The nerves of sensibility that convey to the centre of perception impressions by which the mind is informed of the action of the muscles, &c. These are furnished in small numbers, and hence the muscles possess little sensibility. None of these nerves can be concerned in imparting to the muscle its vital properties. Those belong to the vitality of the muscle, and this can only be maintained by supplies of blood, requiring the integrity of all the nerves

194. The muscles are divided into two classes—those of voluntary and involuntary motion. The former are also called the muscles of animal life, and the latter of organic life. The muscles of animal life invest the bones, are mostly on the outer parts of the body, and abound in the limbs. The muscles of voluntary motion belong to the vascular system, and the digestive and respiratory apparatus. Some of the muscles of voluntary motion attach to the bones, but most terminate their extremities in a fibrous arrangement of sellular tissue called tendon, and by these tendons are attached to the bones. Some suppose the tendons are formed by the continuation of the sheaths which surround the muscular fibres (170).

195. In their texture the tendons differ little from ligaments. They are composed of small fibres closely united, and are surrounded by a sheath, lined by a membrane which secretes for them a lubricating fluid. They possess little elasticity, have no sensibility, and few vessels. Like the cartilage and ligaments, they are soft in early life, and rigid in age.

196. The tendons, attached to the muscles at one end, adhere at the other to the periosteum, or membrane which surrounds and unites them to the bones; thus they become the media through which the muscles act on the bones. Some are long, and extend to parts considerably removed from the muscles, as in the upper and lower extremities. This arrangement secures many mechanical advantages, and contributes to the symmetry of the body, by accumulating muscles into masses in some places and withdrawing them from others, thereby giving the outlines of the trunk, limbs, ankles, wrists, &c. The tendons are usually found at the extremities of muscles, but are sometimes inserted in the middle, dividing the muscle, as in the under jaw, the neck, diaphragm, &c. The end of the muscle attached to the most fixed point is its head or origin; the fleshy mass is the body, and the end attached to the movable point is its termination. Some of the muscles are only attached at one extremity; and some, being circular, have no direct attachment to the bones. Both kinds are in the face, surrounding the mouth, &c.

197. As the muscles have only the power to produce emotion by their contraction, they are arranged to act as antagonists to each other, some *dis*placing a part and some *re*placing it: some bending a limb and some extending it: and, therefore, they are termed abductor and adductor—the flexor and extensor muscles. The flexor muscles are more powerful than the extensors, and hence, when the WILL ceases to act, the limbs are partially fixed or bent.

198. According to Meckel, "There are in the normal or proper state of the body two hundred and thirty-eight different muscles, six of which are composed of two parts which unite on the median line, and two hundred and thirty-two are in pairs; so that the whole number of the voluntary muscles are four hundred and seventy." These are so arranged that by the contraction of the different pairs or muscles all motions are performed. The function of respiration, which is both voluntary and involuntary, employs some of these muscles.

199. The muscles of involuntary motion are much more simple than those of animal life; and, except in the heart, have no appearance of tendons. Their fibres are not parallel, but interlace, and are much shorter than those of the voluntary muscles. They are arranged in layers, and these are generally transverse or oblique, forming rings round the cavities which they circumscribe.

The circular fibres are nearest each other at the orifices of the cavities, and are stronger than the longitudinal fibres. The involuntary muscles do not act in opposition, but either in concert or so as to counteract each other, as their office is to diminish the cavities. Some of the muscles, however, act alternately, as in the heart and intestines. The involuntary muscles are even more abundantly supplied with vessels than those of animal life.

200. The muscles, like the cartilages, ligaments, tendons, &c., are at first very soft, and gradually become more consistent and rigid.

201. Muscular substance once destroyed is never reproduced; but when muscles are wounded the breach is healed and the parts united by a peculiar arrangement of cellular tissue, which is insensible to stimulants.

V.

202. The nervous system is the most interesting portion of the body. It is the immediate organism of vitality, and the intellectual manifestation; hence the nervous system constitutes the man.

204. By the vital powers of the nerves the functions of all the organs are performed. The food is digested into chyme, chyle, blood, the solids and fluids, and the temperature of the body is regulated (173).

205. By the nerves we perceive our wants, conditions, and relations; and by virtue of the nervous substances we think, reason, feel, and act, as intellectual and moral beings.

208. Drawing its nourishment from the earth, the tree is fixed to the spot from which it springs. And, so far as those vital operations by which chyme, chyle, and blood are produced, and organic life sustained, the animal differs little from the vegetable.

209. The zoophytes approach so near to vegetables that naturalists long doubted whether they belong to the animal or vegetable kingdom. They are nourished by means which scarcely demand faculties superior to those with which the vegetable is endowed. But the higher animals require a perception of the wants of the system, and the faculties by which they can seize the substances by which those wants are supplied. Hence organs of sensation and locomotion are necessary, the office of which is to procure the materials by which the system is sustained in its operations, and also to withdraw from those causes by which the vital interests may be destroyed.

210. There are, therefore, in organised bodies, two classes of functions, and a corresponding organisation: the primary, concerned in the nourishment of the body as an organised being; the secondary, of functions which minister to the primary with reference to the relations between those internal wants and the external supplies.

211. The question is, Do the functions common to all organised bodies depend on a system of nerves, or are they performed independently of any nervous system?

213. The nervous system has been considered as consisting of the brain and spinal marrow, with their numerous branches; and these have been supposed to preside over all the operations of life.

214. Some have contended that the brain is the point from which spring the spinal trunk and branches of the nervous system, and considered the brain as the centre of nervous as well as sensorial power. The opinion generally entertained, however, is, that the spinal marrow is the centre of the

nervous system, and that the brain and nervous branches spring from it. But if either of these opinions were correct, the brain or spinal marrow would be the first-formed portion of the system ; for it is a law of nature that those parts are first produced which are essential to the earliest operations. In the establishment of an economy by which an animal body is to be developed, the first thing is a presiding centre; next the blood-vessels, over which that centre presides, and by which the development of the other parts is effected. If the brain or spinal marrow were the presiding centre in the formative processes of the body, it would follow that the branches would issue from it, and go out with the blood-vessels to preside in the formation of other parts. But so far is the brain or spinal marrow from being the first-formed portion of the system, that all the other parts are formed while the brain and spinal marrow are yet in a fluid state, incapable of exercising functional power ; and so far are the nervous branches supposed to issue from the spinal marrow from investing the blood-vessels, that they are almost totally distributed to the voluntary muscles and surface of the body.

215. Nature has not left us in the dark on these points. Where her normal operations have failed to instruct, her abnormal have afforded demonstration. Children have been born without a vestige of brain or spinal marrow ; and I have known one instance in which all the parts were regularly developed except that there was no brain nor spinal marrow, nor a trace of a spinal canal—the vertebræ being solid. Such children cannot live after respiration becomes necessary ; because respiration, though involuntary, is connected with the nerves and muscles of animal life.

216. Some, because they could not tear the brain and spinal marrow from the animal without arresting life, have insisted that those organs preside over these functions. But ten thousand such experiments are of no weight against the fact that nature has produced a body in all other respects perfect, but destitute of brain and spinal marrow.

217. It follows that the brain and spinal marrow stand rather in the relation of an effect than a cause to the formative operations of the system ; and either this economy has no nervous system which presides over its functions, or there is a system of nerves independent of the brain and spinal marrow.

218. In the body such a system is found. In the midst of those parts, first in the order of development (174) is a mass of nervous matter which resembles the brain ; this mass, undoubtedly first formed in the centre, which presides over the functions concerned in the development of the body, and of nutrition during life.

219. In connection with this mass is produced the rudiment of a heart, with a few blood-vessels, which gradually become more complex. Into these enter branches from the central mass, which through life presides over the functions of the sanguiferous system. Accompanying the blood-vessels, other branches go from the central brain and form subordinate brains, which become centres of development to individual organs. These subordinate centres give off branches, some of which enter the blood-vessels appropriated in the construction of their particular organs ; others are distributed to the muscles of those organs, others as the conductors of impressions made upon the organs ; and to establish a more intimate connection between the different centres, large

cords run from one to another, and interlace with branches coming from other special centres and the great common centre.

220. The alimentary canal and organs associated in the function of nutrition being earlier in development than other parts (174), the special centres of action to them are the first subordinate brains the formative economy produces. At an early stage fibres rise on each side of the mass, which form a pair of large cords, called the trisplanchnic nerves, that pass upwards on the right and left of the middle line, and give rise to small brains, which gradually separate, keeping up their connection by branches, till they form a range of fifteen little brains on each side, extending along the spinal column from the bottom of the thoracic cavity to the top of the neck. The trisplanchnic nerves become divided in their upper portions into from three to seven branches, which terminate in as many of the little brains. Eight or nine more of these are arranged on each side in the abdominal cavity, so as to form a continued series from the base of the cranium to the extremity of the spinal column. Each little brain sends out branches, some of which serve to unite the several centres; others plunge into the muscles, and others form connections with the nerves and muscles of animal life. But the largest number of branches go to interlace and form plexuses with others and the great central mass. From these plexuses, again, branches are given off to the different organs entering into their texture. And all the branches, as they proceed, cross, unite, and interlace, so as to form one extended net, the meshes of which become smaller as the nerves approach their minute termination in the organs.

221. The two ranges of little brains, with their cords and branches, are supposed to bring the parts associated in the functions of organic life into union, and establish between them powerful sympathy, and, therefore, are called the great sympathetic nerves. Some, however, include under this denomination all the nerves of organic life. But there has been much error on this point. Whatever may be the knowledge concerning these nerves, most writers on anatomy still speak of the brain or spinal marrow as the grand centre of nervous power which presides over the functions of organic life, as well as those of animal life; and, therefore, they do not perceive any other use for the nerves of organic life than sympathetic association.

222. That the series of little brains, with their cords, &c., bring the organs with which they are connected into union, and establish a bond of sympathy, is true, and I consider it equally certain that they perform other important offices.

223. Considering this system of nerves as that which presides over the vital functions in the sustenance of the body, and the other special centres described as being concerned in the development of the organs of nutrition, does it not follow from analogy, as well as from anatomical arrangement, that the series which extend the length of the spinal column are concerned in the development of the spinal nerves and cerebro-spinal system, and perhaps the other parts pertaining to the trunk and extremities?

224. It seems to be a law of the vital economy that, where any new centre is established for any organ, a subordinate brain or nervous ganglion is produced. One of these ganglions is found on each spinal nerve, near its connection with the spinal marrow; several are found in the brain, and the

spinal marrow itself is but a continued series of them. If the spinal nerves are not developed from the spinal marrow, but by the nerves of organic life (223), where does their development commence, if not at the ganglions near the spinal marrow? And is this not rendered more probable by the fact that each of these ganglions is connected with one of the little brains of organic life?

225. We perceive, then, that by cords which unite the little brains to the central mass, and to each other, and the branches from the centres, which form plexuses in the cavities of the body, these centres are brought into intimate union, as a single system; and then, by branches from each of these centres to its particular organ, and which pass from the plexuses to different organs, the whole is woven into one grand web of nervous tissue.

226. I have said (218) that the central mass resembles the brain. This is also true of all the special centres. Like the brain, they are composed of white and grey nervous substance, surrounded by a membrane, analogous to the pia-mater (272), and an envelope of cellular tissue. They have the closest resemblance to the brain of some of the lower animals; and they perform many of the functions of a brain, acting as centres in receiving impressions and dispensing nervous powers to their special domains. In anatomy, these bodies are termed ganglions. The central mass consists of two semicircular bodies about an inch long and half an inch broad, lying on the right and left side of the backbone, called the semilunar ganglions. They are, probably, at first, united in a single mass (281), and remain closely connected by large branches, which form the solar plexus. These semilunar ganglions, united by the solar plexus, constitute the grand centre of all the ganglions and plexuses of organic life

227. The ganglions of organic life are divided into two orders, the central and the peripheral or limiting ganglions. The central are deeply seated among the viscera, and preside over the functions concerned in nourishing the body; the peripheral form the two ranges on the sides of the spinal column, appropriated to the sympathies of the system, called the sympathetic nerves (221).

228. This system of nerves (225) is sometimes called the ganglionic system. And, because these preside over the functions common to animals and vegetables (208), and, in health, without the consciousness of the animal, they are also called the nerves of vegetative life, but commonly the nerves of organic life, in contradistinction to the brain and spinal marrow, with their branches, &c., which are called the nerves of animal life

229. There seems to be little propriety in calling these latter the nerves of animal life, for they have no independent *life*, nor are they directly concerned in maintaining the common life of the body. Their functions may be suspended for a considerable time, and still the common vitality be preserved. Andrew Wallace, who has since died at the age of 105 years, was struck down by lightning, soon after the close of the American Revolution, and lay seventeen days in a state of suspended consciousness; and a youth, now living in Philadelphia, once lay twenty-eight days in this condition. But a moment's suspension of the nerves of organic life would be death, from which there can be no resuscitation. The brain and spinal marrow, &c., are also called the phrenic nerves, as being the immediate instruments of the mind, but, properly, the cerebro-spinal nerves.

230. Of the nerves of organic life there are three orders (219). First, those that enter the blood-vessels, in their ramifications, and preside over their functions of absorption, circulation, secretion, structure, &c. ; second, those that go to the muscles of involuntary motion in the organs, and convey the stimulus of motion ; third, those distributed to the organs, as the nerves of organic sensation, which convey to the special centres and the common centre (226) the impressions made upon the organs.

231. In this distribution each organ is supplied according to its function. The heart, which in its rudimental state lies near the ganglionic centre (219), and is employed in constructing the alimentary canal and organs (220), is gradually removed farther from the centre as the parts become developed. Employed as a mechanical power, to circulate the blood without effecting any changes in it, the heart seems to possess but few nerves ; neither do the large blood-vessels ; but in the minute extremities of the vessels, where important changes take place, the nerves largely abound. The stomach is remarkable for its nervous endowment, and for its sympathetic relations. Lying near the ganglionic centre it receives a large supply of nerves from that source, and is brought into sympathetic union with all parts in its domain, also with the heart, liver, lungs, &c.

233. The cerebro-spinal nerves are exclusively organs of external relation (214-215), nor are they essential to life until respiration and deglutition become necessary. The introduction of substances into the lungs and stomach, and the voluntary evacuations, are the only duties they perform in the processes of nutrition.

235. The cerebro-spinal nerves originate with the parts to which they belong, and in the progress of the general development become connected with the spinal and cerebal centres. Whether vegetables have nerves or not, we know that the economy by which they are developed has a single starting-point, the centre of action ; and this is also true in the development of animal bodies. A centre of unity is first established: this (226) is the central brain of the nerves of organic life, consisting of the semilunar ganglions and solar plexus, and from this all the subordinate centres, branches, &c., are developed by the blood-vessels over which these nerves preside (219). But portions of these, acting by special centres (219), may commence the structure of different parts in a measure independent of each other (174), just as ossification commences at points which have no connection, while they depend upon a single economy. In this manner the cerebro-spinal nerves originate in several parts, and, by subsequent connection, constitute a single system. Hence (215), the spinal nerves may be developed without a spinal marrow, and the spinal nerves and marrow may be developed without a brain. Even the brain has been developed without a spinal marrow.

236. The order of development in the cerebro-spinal system is probably as follows :—1. The spinal nerves arising from the spinal marrow. The development of these (224) probably commences at the ganglions near the spine. 2. The spinal marrow. 3. Those ganglions of the brain essential to taste, smell, hearing, and sight, together with the special nerves by which these functions are performed. 4. The ganglions which constitute the organism of the mental and moral faculties. And 5. The cerebral hemispheres themselves.

237. Having pointed out the order of development, I proceed to a description of the cerebro-spinal system of nerves, as they present themselves to the eye of the anatomist.

238. The spinal marrow lies in the hollow of the backbone (180-182). It appears when examined to be composed of white and grey nervous substance (161), the grey situated internally, somewhat like a series of ganglions, and surrounded by the white. It is divided into a right and left half, each of which consists of a front and back column, so that the whole is composed of two pairs. The two front portions correspond in form and character, and the two back in like manner, thus constituting a double spinal marrow, as if the two halves had a distinct existence, which, indeed, is really the case ; for one side may be paralysed while the other remains in possession of its powers.

239. The spinal marrow is enveloped in three membranes. The first is full of blood-vessels to nourish it, hence called the *pia-mater*, or natural mother. The second, called the arachnoid, or spider's-web membrane, is extremely thin, and moistened by its own serous exhalation. The third, or lining of the canal, is a strong fibrous membrane, called the *dura-mater*, or hard mother (169).

240. Connected with the marrow, on each side of the canal, are thirty pairs of nerves, called the spinal nerves. Each consists of filaments, surrounded by the *pia-mater* and an envelope resembling the *dura-mater*.

241. As the nerves on each side are alike, it is convenient to describe them on one only ; but when I speak of a nerve it is one of a pair, the corresponding one being on the opposite side.

242. Part of the filaments which compose each spinal nerve rise from the back portion, and a part from the front of the spinal marrow. Those from the back run into a ganglion, and, proceeding, unite with those from the front, and form the cord to be dispersed over the body. But in entering into the cord the filaments retain their character, and are again, ultimately, separated. The filaments from the back of the spinal marrow are the nerves of sensation. Some are distributed to the muscles, and endow those organs with a small degree of sensibility, by which the mind is informed of the action of the muscles, and enabled to regulate the extent of the action. The rest of the posterior filaments proceed to the skin, and constitute a general organ of touch—the faculty of external relation. They abound more in some parts than others, making portions of the body the special organs of touch.

243. The filaments which arise from the front of the spinal marrow are the nerves of motion. They are distributed to the muscles (194), ramifying over the system. These convey stimulus, causing the muscles to contract in obedience to the will. If the filaments from the back of the spinal marrow be separated from that centre, the sensibility of the parts to which they are distributed is destroyed ; the centre of perception has no longer cognizance of any sensation, yet the power of motion will remain. But if the filaments from the front be separated, the power of motion will be lost, while sensibility remains.

244. The spinal marrow continues upward and extends into the cranium Near its entrance its two lateral parts divide into cords, which cross so that those from the right side take the left, and those from the left the right . and

they are enlarged by masses of grey substance (161). The head of the spinal marrow is divided into three pairs of bodies : two in front, the pyramidal ; two behind, the restiform ; and two at the sides, called olivary bodies. These last are principally grey substance, surrounded by a thin layer of white. Besides, there is a strip lying between the restiform and olivary bodies, extending between the anterior and posterior portions of the spinal marrow (238), which gives origin to the nerves associated in the function of respiration. These bodies are so united as to form a single bulb, called the medulla oblongata.

245. From the sides of this bulb rise several pairs of nerves, and from its top all the other parts within the cranium.

In the neck, branches from different nerves unite to form a nerve which descends to the diaphragm, and is concerned in respiration. In its course it gives off twigs, which unite with ganglionic nerves of the neck, branches from the solar plexus, and other nerves. This nerve belongs to the respiratory apparatus, which ordinarily acts without the will, but which the will can control. The next nerve above, called the spinal accessory, has an extended origin. Some of its roots arise from the lower part of the neck, others from the middle and upper part. These enter the skull with the spinal marrow, and, after receiving roots from the medulla oblongata, form a cord which is distributed to the muscles concerned in moving the breast, collar bones, and shoulder blade, and drawing back the head and shoulders. Of those nerves which have their origin within the skull the lowest is the hypoglossal. It arises by roots from the groove between the pyramidal and olivary bodies, passes out at the base of the skull, and, after giving off twigs and receiving others, it divides into branches, distributed to the tongue, imparting motion in mastication, swallowing, speaking, singing, &c. The next above is called the pneumo-gastric, or lungs-and-stomach nerve. It arises by roots near the top of the medulla oblongata, and from the strip between the restiform and olivary bodies. It issues with the spinal accessory, and by branches forms connections with almost every nerve in the throat, neck, and thoracic cavity. It has been called the middle sympathetic. It sends branches to the pharynx, the meat-pipe, the larynx, and the windpipe; also branches which unite with others from the sympathetic, to form the cardiac plexus. These different branches interweave, so as to bring the throat and neck into direct relations. Several branches also enter into plexuses for the lungs, and some extend to the solar plexus, the plexus of the liver, spleen, &c.; but the main body descends to the stomach, interweaving with nerves from the great centre of organic life.

247. In the stomach the pneumogastric is not a nerve of common sensibility, while its branches in the membrane of the larynx and windpipe appear to be highly sensible. It appears to occupy a middle ground between the nerves of organic and animal life ; in its origin a nerve of sensation and motion, and after, associated with the nerves of organic life, becomes an animo-organic nerve, giving motion perhaps to the bronchæ and to the stomach, in vomiting, &c.; also constituting the medium by which the centre of perception has cognizance of hunger, thirst, and the desire for air ; and the brain and stomach are brought into sympathy.

248. The next is the glossopharangeal, or tongue-and-pharynx nerve. It rises by filaments from the groove between the restiform and olivary bodies, above the pneumogastric. It gives off branches, which unite with other nerves, and supply parts in the throat, but mainly the pharynx and tongue. Another rises immediately above, called the facial nerve. It passes out near the ear, to the muscles of the face: the chin, lips, angles of the mouth, cheeks, nostrils, eyelids, eyebrows, forehead, ears, neck, &c., uniting with the branches of several other nerves. The next is the abductor, or external muscular nerve of the eye. It rises from the top of the pyramidal body, passes out at the back of the cavity for the eyeball, and goes to the muscles which turn the eye outward. This nerve is entirely appropriated to voluntary motion. There are six other pairs, which originate within the cranium, all of which rise from the top of the medulla oblongata; but their roots are so covered that they have the appearance of springing from parts removed from that point.

249. The nerve which next presents itself is the auditory, and the next the trifacial, both of which I shall leave for the present. The internal motor nerve of the eye is the smallest within the cranium. This goes to the muscle which rolls the eye, turns the pupil downward and outward, and gives the pathetic expression to the eye—hence it is called the pathetic. The common motor nerve of the eye rises by filaments, traced back nearly to the top of the medulla oblongata. The filaments form the nerve, which is distributed to the muscles of the eye, to direct the pupil towards the object of vision.

250. The nerves which remain are those of special sense, and the trifacial. These have their origin near the head of the medulla oblongata (236). The quadrigeminal bodies are four small ganglions lying at the top. A little removed from these are the two largest ganglions of the brain, called the optic thalami, supposed to give rise to the optic nerves; and two smaller ganglions, called the striated bodies. These are composed of grey substance (161), traversed by white or medullary fibres, and lie near the base of the brain.

251. Anatomists have attempted to demonstrate the points at which the olfactory, optic, and auditory nerves rise from these bodies. As they are traced towards their origin, they become less distinct till they fade into the substance of the parts from which they rise.

252. The auditory nerves are endowed with the power of receiving sounds, and are distributed to the cavities of the ear. The olfactory nerves, receiving smell, are distributed over the cavities of the nose. The optic nerve terminates in a delicate expansion, called the retina, which surrounds the humours of the eye, receiving sight. It is always present where vision exists.

253. The nerves of special sense have no tactile sensibility. The optic nerve is no more sensible to laceration than a dead tree, but is delicately sensible to light, which we can in no other manner perceive. Nor is there the least foundation for the notion that other nerves may perform the functions of these. The sense of touch is as truly special as that of sight, hearing, smell, or taste. It is more extensive in its organism than any other, because the relations of the animal require it; but the extensiveness does not render the sense less specific. If the optic nerve were expanded over the surface of the body, so that the animal could see at every point, the optic would be no less a special sense.

254. The trifacial nerve is the largest within the cranium, and in many respects corresponds with the spinal nerves. Its posterior root, coming from the restiform body, is composed of thirty or forty fasciculi, containing about a hundred filaments, which interlace to form the gasserian ganglion. This portion is endowed with sensibility. The anterior portion which arises from the pyramidal body does not enter the ganglion. This is the motor portion of the nerve, and is distributed to the muscles concerned in mastication, &c. From the gasserian ganglion the nerve proceeds in three branches, called the ophthalmic, the superior and inferior maxillary. The ophthalmic is distributed to the eye, giving sensibility to the ball, &c. The superior maxillary is distributed to the upper part of the face, roof of the mouth, gum, lip, root of each tooth, &c. The inferior maxillary is distributed to the lower parts of the face, mouth, ear, teeth, gum, tongue, lip, chin, &c. It also gives rise to the branch which is endowed with the power of receiving taste, and is distributed by filaments to the mouth and throat, particularly upon the edges of the tongue ; thus forming the organ of taste. The trifacial unites with the facial nerve, &c., and with a number of twigs from the sympathetic. It communicates with the organs of all the five senses, and brings these parts into a direct relation with the stomach and domain of organic life.

260. We see, that the spinal marrow and nerves, together with the medulla oblongata and nerves within the cranium, are the agents of sensation, perception, and motion. The brain itself is appropriated to the intellectual and moral powers, and has little more to do with the body than to depend on its organic economy for sustenance, and constitute the special organism through which the mind is acted on by, and in turn acts on, the body—directly by the WILL, and indirectly in mental excitements.

VI.

261. The parts within the cranium are collectively called the brain.

262. About the seventh year (214) the brain is supposed to have attained completeness for vigorous exercise ; but at this age continued mental operations are neither safe nor wise.

264. The medulla oblongata (244) leans forward in the cranium, and rests its anterior surface in a groove formed in the basilar bone. This brings the two pyramidal, partially under the restiform, bodies, placed above. Medullary fibres (250), continuing from these last through masses of the grey substance, are reflected backwards, and expanded into peculiar foldings forming the little brain. The fibres from each restiform body form a lobe, so that the little brain consists of two lobes. Some of the fibres unite on the middle line at the top of the medulla oblongata, forming the uniting portion, or bridge, of the little brain, sometimes called the transverse fibres. Several pairs of nerves have the appearance of originating in this body. Besides the transverse fibres, there are others which connect each lobe with the quadrigeminal bodies and the brain proper.

265. The fibres continuing from the pyramidal bodies, together with those from the olivary, and a few from the restiform bodies, proceed through masses

of the grey substance, which are covered by the transverse fibres of the little brain, the olivary fasciculi becoming connected with the quadrigeminal bodies, and form what are called the legs of the brain.   They now plunge into the great ganglions of the brain, called the optic thalami (250).   The pyramidal bodies Spurzheim considers the rudiments of such parts as belong to the intellect; and, in man, the olivary and part of the restiform bodies, as the roots of those that pertain to the affective manifestations.   In accordance with this view, he says that in animals that portion formed by the olivary fasciculi is more voluminous than that formed by the pyramidal, and as we descend in the scale of being its proportion increases; while in man, that formed by the pyramidal fasciculi constitutes two-thirds of each cerebral leg.

269. According to Tiedemann, the medullary fibres that issue from the cerebral ganglions (265), at first form a thin fibrous membrane on each side. These curve their edges towards the middle, gradually meet, and form the corpus callosum, or great cerebral commissure ; by so doing, forming the two hemispheres of the brain, as yet in a membranous state, without any convolutions . but the membrane is thickened by new matter on the surface.   The fibres traced from the medulla oblongata to the corpus callosum are the same that come from the legs of the brain; and were the skull sufficiently capacious for an entire development of the cerebral hemisphere in this form, the brain might come to maturity without a single convolution.   In cases of hydrocephalus, where the hemispheres are expanded, they are brought back into that state.   And this takes place without any disturbance of the function.

271. When the hemispheres are developed, the membrane begins to gather into folds, to still accommodate itself to the skull. The development proceeds, till a membrane is folded with a surface several times greater than that of the skull, the parts becoming so compacted as to give to the surface those elevations called convolutions.   The corpus callosum also is brought down near to the base, and forms the fissure extending between the two halves and the cavities of the hemispheres.

272. Each hemisphere is subdivided into three lobes an anterior in the forehead, a posterior in the back of the head over the little brain, and a middle lobe in the region of the ear.   Each of these, again, is composed of convolutions.   The membrane called the *pia-mater*, which surrounds the spinal marrow (239), comes up and expands over the brain, adhering to the surface, and dipping into every depression.   Over this is spread the arachnoid membrane, which also continues from the spinal marrow ; which, beside covering the cerebrum, forms a sheath for the nerves and vessels which enter the skull ; and, enveloping the whole, the strong membrane called the *dura-mater*, continues up from the spinal canal, lines the inner surface of the skull, dips down, by the faciform process, between the hemispheres to the corpus callosum, forms a partition between the posterior lobes and the little brain, and separates the lobes of the little brain.

280. The nerves of the trunk and extremities, and the nerves within the cranium, converge towards the head of the medulla oblongata (251).   The parts above may be destroyed without destroying the power of sensation and motion ; and below may be paralysed without abolishing the intellectual

powers. It may, therefore, be asserted, that the centre of life is at the top of the medulla oblongata. Here seems to be such a focal point of the nervous machinery that we can put our finger on the whole, and arrest all the functions of this system.

281. I have alluded to the duplicate form of those parts which belong to animal life (238). If the body be divided, it will be found to consist of two corresponding halves : the bones, the muscles, and the nerves of one side correspond with the other. The parts removed from the middle line are in pairs ; as the eyes, ears, extremities, &c. The halves of the cerebro-spinal system are very exact in their resemblance. The right and left half of the brain and spinal marrow are almost alike. Yet this symmetry is less perfect in man than in animals.* This difference is unquestionably a degeneracy in the species, and has resulted from the habits of man.

282. In the domain of organic life, though there is some approach to the duplicate form, yet there is no regularity. The two lungs do not correspond, nor the halves of the heart.

284. When treating of the nerves of organic life, I spoke of a range of ganglions lying on each side of the backbone (220), extending from the skull to the extremity of the spinal column, connected with the centre of organic life, by cords radiating from that centre. There are, on each side, three in the neck, twelve in the back, five in the loins, and three or four in the sacral regions. These ganglions lie near where the spinal nerves of animal life are connected with the spinal marrow ; and each ganglion gives off two branches, which join the corresponding spinal nerve. One branch is larger than the other, and sends twigs to the muscles between the ribs. This is supposed to be the medium of communication from the ganglion to the nerve ; and the other, which gives off no twigs, the medium from the nerve to the ganglion. The ganglions also give off filaments which go with the nerves to the muscles, especially to those concerned in respiration. The highest ganglion lies at the base of the skull, and sends a branch which forms a plexus around the main artery of the brain, passing with it into the cranium, with two or three cerebral nerves, particularly the trifacial. This nerve also, after passing out of the cranium, unites extensively with the nerves of organic life (254). Such are the connections between the ganglions of organic life and the nerves of animal life.

285. The upper central connections are mainly established by the pneumogastric (245) ; (247).

286. Another connection is formed between the two systems by that arrangement on which the body depends for sustenance. The nerves of organic life appropriated to the vascular system, penetrate into every structure. Even the brain, and all the nerves, are nourished by blood-vessels, over which the nerves of organic life preside. By this relation, the nerves of organic life are brought into connection with those of the cerebro-spinal system.

287. A membranous texture of cellular tissue covers the body ; continuing

---

* "Considered either in regard to symmetry or structure," says Meckel, "the nervous system of man is less regular than that of other animals, even those which are nearest to him. In fact, the halves of the nervous system correspond more perfectly in the mammalia, and the deviations from the normal state in those animals are rarer than in man."

over the lips and up the nostrils, the same membrane lines the mouth and nose, covering the tongue, &c., and continuing downward, lines the throat, the windpipe, the air passages and cells, presenting to the air in the lungs an extent of surface equal to the whole external skin. The same membrane continues down the meat-pipe, lining the stomach and the intestinal canal. This membrane is a delicate net-work, with an infinite number of extremely small meshes. Through these penetrate in countless numbers the minute capillary vessels of the sanguiferous and lymphatic systems, with their nerves. Innumerable nerves of sensation pass through the membrane in the same manner. These are so minute that it is not possible to puncture the skin with the finest needle without wounding both a nerve and a blood-vessel. To lubricate these delicate organs, they are everywhere surrounded by thin mucus. This is called the *rete mucosum*, and contains the substance which gives the colour to the skin, being black in the negro, copper-coloured in the Indian, white in white people, &c. Still farther to protect these organs, the external surface is covered with a thin transparent substance called the epidermis or cuticle.

289. The skin, lungs, and alimentary canal resemble each other, in regard to the substances which they throw off from the system; and are vicarious in their offices, the excess of one corresponding with the suppression of another. The internal skin is called the mucous membrane.

290. The myriads of *feelers* in the skin are nerves of animal life, connected with the back portion of the spinal marrow (242), and through it with the top of the medulla oblongata and brain. Those of the mucous membrane are nerves of organic life (230), connected with their centres of perception, and through them with the centre of organic life (226). The nerves of animal sensibility also extend to portions of the mucous membrane which line parts subject to the control of the WILL, as the mouth, throat, &c.

291. Thus the skin constitutes a very extensive medium of connection between the nerves of organic, and those of animal life; and the sympathetic relations are equally powerful. The mucous membrane sympathises directly in the irritations of the skin, and the skin sympathises in the affections of the mucous membrane, particularly in morbid affections.

292. It is important that the meaning of the terms organic, and animal, sensibility should be understood. The large nervous mass at the back of the stomach is the common centre of organic life, the smaller masses being the centres of particular organs; and the head of the spinal marrow is the centre of the nerves of animal life, or external relation.

293. The centres of organic life (219) preside over their particular organs; but, so far as it is associated with the functions of other organs, the centre is confederated with other centres; and, so far as each is related to the common centre as a part of the whole, each special centre is subordinate to the common centre; and, so far as the COMMON WHOLE of organic life requires the exercise of the organs of external relation, it is subordinate to the centre of animal life. The powers of this last centre, then, are : the perception of wants, such as air, food, drink, &c.; the means by which these can be satisfied ; and that influence by which the necessary motions are performed.

c

294. When there is health throughout the body, and every function properly performed, the special centres only have perception of what is taking place in their spheres, while the common centre has perception of the condition of each organ, and presides over the whole domain of organic life. The centre of animal life has no control over the functions of organic life. It only has cognisance of the common wants of the system. The functions of the stomach, intestinal canal, liver, &c., are, in health, no more perceived by the centre of animal life than they would if they belonged to another animal (228). Hence the nerves of organic life have no sensibility. They may be touched, cut, or lacerated, and the animal will suffer no pain, because the centre of perception has no consciousness of the act. But the functions over which the centre of life presides, require that this should have a perception of external things, with their qualities and conditions. Density or resistance, heat, cold, &c., must be *felt*. Hence a part of the nerves (242) are endowed with the power of conveying to the centre of perception impressions ; and, as the qualities in relation to which this exists may injure the body, the sense is universal in the domain of animal life. The skin is supplied with nerves which constitute it a general organ of touch. The internal skin and the muscles also receive a supply. That property of the nerves of animal life, then, which enables us to feel heat and cold, and to know when anything wounds or touches us, and to perceive the qualities of hard, soft, rough, smooth, &c., is what is called sensibility ; and the exercise of this power we call sensation. This is the faculty of external relation (242), and always present when life exists. It is a power which gives the perception of external things (253). But there are qualities of things. which exist in relation to organic life, not perceived by this sense. For the perception of these the animal is endowed with other senses, as taste (254), smell (252), hearing, and sight.

295. Each of these is a power by which the centre of animal life perceives certain qualities, and are never vicarious in their functions (253). The eye never hears, the ear never sees, &c.

296. In the domain of organic life, though we find no animal sensibility, each organ possesses an organic sensibility as delicate as the sensibility of the nose, ear, or eye, and as fitted to appreciate the qualities of things in relation to which it was constituted. Organic sensibility is the power of the nerves of organic life to convey to their centres impressions made by substances contained in the organs, but this sensibility has nice shades of difference, adapted to the purposes of each organ. The sensibility of the stomach is adapted to the properties of food ; that of the intestinal tube to the properties of chyme, &c. ; that of the lacteals to the chyle ; that of the arteries, &c., to the blood ; that of the biliary vessels to the bile, &c. But this adaptation unfits them for improper substances, and when such are introduced they are the causes of irritation and disease.

297. In regard to the sympathetic relations, there is considerable difference between the nerves of organic and animal life. The organs of animal life are comparatively isolated. A hand or foot, an ear or an eye, or even a lobe of the brain, may be destroyed, and the corresponding organs of animal life will suffer little sympathy. But in the domain of organic life all parts sympathise.

If the stomach receives food adapted to the wants of the vital economy it is healthfully excited, its condition is agreeable, and the other organs sympathise, performing their own functions with energy; on the other hand, if, by the ingestion of an improper substance, the stomach is disturbed, the other organs sympathise, and their functions are either accelerated or retarded.

298. The other organs also sympathise with the intestinal canal, with the liver, kidneys, &c. But the degree of influence is proportionate to the importance of the organ. Hence the stomach holds an important station in the assemblage of vital organs. Supplied with nerves from the centre of organic life (231), and with the pneumogastric from the centre of animal life (245, 285), and associated with the surrounding organs, it sympathises more powerfully with every part of the body than any other organ; and, in turn, every part sympathises more directly with the stomach than with any other organ.

299. As the organs of animal life depend on the nerves of organic life which belong to the blood-vessels that enter them for their sustenance, they sympathise directly with the internal organs, particularly the stomach. If the eyes, ears, hands, feet, &c., be diseased, every disturbance of the stomach aggravates that disease; and chronic indigestion impairs the whole system. Few things will more completely prostrate the muscular powers than irritation in the alimentary canal. On the other hand, the internal organs sympathise with those of animal life. Excessive cold retards the internal functions; excessive heat debilitates the stomach and other organs, and tends to cause indigestion, pulmonary disease, &c. In short, every external affection has some sympathetic influence on the internal organs; perhaps the most powerful is that between the stomach and brain. A severe blow upon the head will cause vomiting, and all irritation in the brain proportionably affects the stomach. Irritations of the stomach will cause derangement of the brain, and any irritation therein proportionably affects the brain.

300. This sympathy, adapted to the purposes of vitality, so conducive to enjoyment, may, by long abuses, be converted into the source of intolerable suffering. In a healthy state, if any improper substance be brought within the precincts of vital action, the part, perceiving by its organic sensibility (296) the deleterious substance, gives alarm to its centre, and that takes measures, by increased secretion, &c., to shield its domain from the pernicious effects. If the substance be such as to endanger the system, the special centre gives alarm to the common centre of organic life, and, thence spread throughout, all parts sympathise with the suffering organ, and strive to remove the cause. When the danger is imminent, the energy of organic life is poured upon those muscles concerned in respiration, and vomitings, &c., ensue. The organic instinct acts determinately. But if the disturbing cause be continued or frequently repeated, the organic sensibility of the part becomes diseased, the irritability is propagated throughout, and a morbid sympathy is established. The organic instinct thus frequently pours its energy on parts whose action cannot afford relief, and spasms and convulsions are produced. These are generally attributed to irritation of the brain. But I am convinced that this is a capital error, and has been the source of immense evil in therapeutics.

The brain *may be* the seat of those irritations which cause spasms and convulsions, but not necessarily. Convulsive fits and spasmodic affections almost universally result from irritations in the domain of organic life; and the alimentary canal is most generally the seat of those irritations. When the convulsions are continued, the brain becomes sympathetically involved, and suffers ruinously, even to derangement and decay of its substance. Yet how often do we see spasms and convulsions where there is not the slightest symptom of cerebral irritation! proving that the morbid irritations of the nerves of organic life can be transmitted to the muscles of animal life without the cerebro-spinal centre. The numerous branches which the ganglions on each side of the backbone send to the muscles of animal life (284) are probably the media through which the irritations are transmitted.

301. The nerves of organic life (294) are, in health, destitute of animal sensibility, but (296) endowed with organic sensibility; and the integrity of their functions depends on the nerves. But the organic sensibility of these nerves may become diseased. In this state of things the functions are impaired to an extent proportionate to the degree of irritability. The food is less digested, the chyle less perfectly elaborated, the blood becomes deteriorated, and the whole system suffers. By irritation, also, inflammation may be induced, and painful sensibility developed in the nerves of organic life; so that the centre of animal life will not only be conscious of the pain, but refer it to the part diseased, the same as it does impressions of its own domain. This is not only distressing, but often hazardous to life. When we are *conscious* that we have a stomach or a liver, from any *feeling* in those organs, something is wrong; for in a healthy state we have no other consciousness of the domain of organic life than appertains to the wants of the vital economy, which require food, drink, air, &c. When food is swallowed, it has passed the cognisance of animal life, to be converted into chyme, chyle, blood, bone, muscle, nerve, &c., all without consciousness.

302. The centre of organic life presides over the functions concerned in nourishing the body (218), and these are removed from the control of the WILL. The stomach, liver, heart, &c., perform their functions without control. But the voluntary powers fulfil external relations, and prevent the ingress of improper substances to the lungs and stomach, the WILL being, as it were, a warden to those organs. The WILL can suspend respiration for a short time, and can exert its power on the respiratory muscles, to accelerate their action. By a control of the respiratory apparatus we are enabled to speak, sing, &c. Yet respiration is properly involuntary, and performed independently of the WILL.

303. The ordinary operations of the mind have little effect upon the nerves of organic life. But when the exercises are intense, the whole domain sympathises with the brain; and when these are impassioned the influence is poured with energy upon the nerves of organic life, and the functions are disturbed, while sensation is produced in the epigastric centre, usually referred to the heart: but the stomach is the true seat of it, this organ being more affected than any other. Indeed, it is in a considerable measure through the stomach that the other organs are affected by mental influence.

304. All mental excitements are causes of disturbance to the nerves of organic life, and induce morbid irritability, generally involving the brain and spinal marrow.

305. The mind sympathises with the nerves of organic life in all their conditions. When this system is in health, every organ performs its function with tone and alacrity. In this there is no *local feeling*, no sensation *in any particular part*. The mind feels the exhilaration, but it is not conscious of its nature. Thoughts flow with ease; imagination becomes vivid, and memory clear; but the mind is not conscious that this is connected with the body. This sympathy between the nervous system of organic life and the mind may be preserved through life. While these nerves are healthy, the mind is cheerful, as in childhood. Moral causes may give pain, but as soon as the action of those causes ceases, it springs elastic from the oppression. When, by irritations of the stomach, &c., the nerves become diseased, and a morbid sympathy established, the mind loses its serenity, and becomes shrouded in pensiveness, followed by discontent—a continual restlessness. We are unhappy, yet we know not why. We long for relief, but we know not what. We would go, but know not where. We would cease to be what we are, yet know not what we would be.

306. Such are the relations between the mind and the nerves of organic life. Peculiarities, which we call hereditary, are transmitted from parent to child through the medium of this system, such as temperament, predisposition to disease; also mental and moral predispositions.

VII.

313. The internal organs are divided into *vessels* and *viscera*. The vessels, as arteries, veins, lymphatics, &c., are called the *vascular system;* and the minute extremities of the arteries and veins, which, with the lymphatics, compose a large portion of the body, are called the *capillary system*. The stomach, liver, pancreas, spleen, intestinal tube, &c., are the *viscera*, or singly a *viscus*. A *function* is the office an organ performs. And the VITAL ECONOMY consists of the co-operation of the organs in the sustenance of the body.

314. In the course of a few years, all the matter in the body undergoes a change. Foreign matter is continually assimilated and incorporated; and organised matter decomposed and eliminated. All bodies are adapted to this condition. They have organs which assimilate, distribute, and convert matter into the various structures of the body, and organs which decompose and convey the worn-out matter from the vital domain.

317. All animals possess a cavity for the digestion of food, yet differ widely in the construction of their alimentary apparatus; each species being adapted to its appropriate aliment.

319. In animals that subsist on food rapidly digested, which requires a quick passage, the stomach is simple, and the alimentary tube short and small; while in those that feed on substances which contain little nutriment, and are slowly digested, the canal is much longer, and has capacious enlargements, or the stomach and colon are constructed to retain their contents a considerable time. In a third class, which subsist on a more nutritious

aliment, as the farinaceous seeds, grains, roots, &c., and fruits, the alimentary tube is longer than that of the first class, and shorter than that of the second ; but its capacity is large, and the stomach and colon are fitted for a slow passage of their contents.

321. In other portions of the alimentary apparatus animals differ as widely as they do in the internal cavity. Some simply imbibe liquid ; some swallow substances which readily dissolve ; others harder substances, mashed by an internal apparatus ; and others have organs with which they masticate their food. The masticatory organs differ again. Some are fitted to tear flesh, others to crop grass and grind woody fibre, others to cut and mash bulbous roots or fruits which constitute their appropriate aliment.

322. The alimentary apparatus of man consists of masticatory organs, a meatpipe, a stomach, an alimentary tube several times the length of the body, together with various glands, vessels, &c.

323. The oral cavity is formed by the bones of the head and face, united by cartilages, bound together by ligaments, and invested by muscles and membranes. The upper jaw is attached to the skull, and only moves with the head. The lower jaw is separate, somewhat of the form of a horseshoe, and attached to the temporal bones by a peculiar joint, which admits of free up-and-down, and also lateral, motion performed in chewing, talking, &c., by several pairs of muscles. Each jaw is composed of an external and internal plate of bone, and an intermediate substance which is spongy. In this are the cavities which contain the roots of the teeth. The gum is a dense cellular tissue, which surrounds the neck of each tooth, affording a firm support.

324. Two front teeth in the lower jaw are the first that appear, about the seventh month after birth, followed by two in the upper jaw; to these succeed two outer front teeth of each jaw ; and then the first molar or double teeth ; then the eye or corner teeth ; and lastly the second double teeth. So that, in three years the twenty temporary teeth appear.

325. The process of second dentition commences about the sixth or seventh year. The permanent teeth are developed in the same manner, and appear in the same order; and as they advance the roots of the first teeth are gradually absorbed, till nothing is left but the part above the gums, which is easily removed.

326. The last of the permanent or "wisdom" teeth do not appear till about the twentieth year. When all are developed, there are two front, one corner, and five cheek teeth, in each half of both jaws, making in the whole thirty-two. The front teeth have single roots, and chisel-shaped crowns for cutting, and are called the incisors. The corner teeth, are the first step of transition from the chisel-shaped cutters to the square mashers ; they, therefore, take more of the round-pointed shape than the front teeth. They are therefore called cuspids (spear-shaped), but more commonly the eye teeth. The first two cheek teeth have the form of two corner teeth united, hence they are called the bicuspids, or two-pointed teeth. The remaining teeth have the form of two bicuspids, or four corner teeth united. The crowns are square, with four or five slight elevations. These are called the molars or grinders.

327. The enamel which covers the crown of each tooth to the edge of the

gum is far the hardest substance in the body, a species of *organic crystallisation*. This does not appear to be reproduced after the tooth is developed; but it sustains the friction of mastication for many years.

330. The skin and mucous membrane (288) constitutes the confines of the vital domain, and through it must pass everything that enters into or egresses from that domain. If fluid is required to enter, this membrane must absorb it. If there be an excess of aqueous matter, this membrane must eliminate it from the system. If nutrient matter is to enter, organs in this membrane must elaborate it. And if substances such as saliva, pancreatic fluid, bile, &c., are to be secreted, this membrane must furnish the organs for the performance of these wonderful functions.

331. The capillary vessels of the sanguiferous and lymphatic systems pass through the skin and mucous membrane (287). Some of these minute vessels are employed in absorbing such substances as pass into the vital domain with little or no change. These abound in the mucous membrane of the alimentary and respiratory cavities, especially in the stomach and alimentary tube. Others are employed in throwing off like substances in the state of vapour, &c. These mostly abound in the lungs and external skin. Another set secrete the nutrient matter by which the system is sustained. These abound in the alimentary cavity, especially the small intestines.

333. The remaining functions connected with the enveloping membrane appear to be performed by more complicated organs; yet they are scarcely less simple than those described. The glandular follicles are little bottle-shaped sacs imbedded in the membrane, their mouths opening on its surface. The sacs possess a contractile tissue, by which they expel their contents. These cluster more in some parts than others. Apparently similar in structure, they differ in their functions. Some secrete mucus (287); others the unctuous matter which oils the skin, said to be not less than a hundred and twenty millions; others the wax of the ears.

334. The next form of gland is much more extensive. Instead of the sac, the membrane forms a tube like a small quill: this gives off branches, and each branch divides into a number of twigs, all hollow and formed by the same mucous membrane; so that the twigs open into the branches, the branches into the main tube, and this upon the face of the membrane. This tube is more or less extensive according to the size of the gland; but only differs from the little sacs in shape and extensiveness. To complete the gland, an artery divides into branches and twigs, which terminate in the membrane; and where these arterial twigs terminate an equal number of venous twigs arise, which run together corresponding with the artery. With these are also associated lymphatic vessels; and all these capillary arteries, veins, and lymphatics are supplied with nerves of organic life (231), and woven together into a single organ by cellular tissue; the whole enveloped in a serous membrane, and the gland completed.

335. This is a description of the salivary glands, the pancreas, the liver, &c. The secretion of the gland takes place in a manner of which we are ignorant; an effect of vitality which seems to possess the power of transmuting one substance into another (51): for many of the secretions are unlike anything

to be found in the blood. These glands are situated in different parts of the body—a number of them in the alimentary cavity—so that the membrane which covers the body and lines all the cavities is one extended organ of secretion, excretion, absorption, and depuration.

338. The mucous membrane is the seat of the processes of alimentation, secretion, excretion, respiration, &c. Having lined the mouth and nasal cavities it unites in the throat, and descending, forms a funnel-shaped cavity called the pharynx, which tapers into a tube. This tube, called the œsophagus, having entered a small opening of the diaphragm, expands into the stomach, which has somewhat the shape of a pear, and lies across the upper part of the abdominal cavity. It is capable of containing from one to two quarts, but may be enlarged by gluttony, and dimimished by disease. It diminishes in size as it proceeds towards the right side, where it contracts into a tube larger than the œsophagus. This tube is six or eight times the length of the body, and folded into a small compass. It is divided into three parts, called the *duodenum*, the *jejunum*, and the *ileum;* more properly, as a whole, the small intestine. This expands into the colon, which is much more capacious. The colon ascends to the stomach, arches over the small intestine, and descends on the left, assuming the shape of an S, and then enters the rectum.

339. Throughout the mucous membrane some of its little vessels. (331) exhale an aqueous fluid, and its glandular follicles secrete a lubricating mucus, to keep its myriads of delicate organs (287) in a proper state, and protect them from the injurious action of substances introduced.

340. In the upper jaw, on each side, the mucous membrane forms a tube which branches into a gland (334) in front of the ear. Another gland lies within the under jaw, on each side ; and a third pair lie under the tongue. These are the salivary glands. They secrete the saliva or solvent fluid during mastication, and whenever any substance is taken into the mouth. The oral cavity (338) continues back into the funnel-shaped pharynx. Into this last open also the canals from the nose, and little tubes from the chambers of the ear, called Eustachian tubes. In front of these is the soft pendulous veil of the palate. This, in the act of swallowing, closes the nasal and Eustachian tubes, so that nothing can pass into them. A little lower opens the *larynx*, or mouth of the windpipe. To prevent food or drink from entering the windpipe, a small valve is placed over the orifice. But as respiration requires that the windpipe should only be momentarily closed, this valve, called the *epiglottis*, is always raised, except during the act of swallowing.

341. The œsophagus does not enter the stomach at its end, or in the line of its longitudinal axis, but at its upper side, so that the mouth of the stomach, which opens into the small intestine, is a little lower than the cardiac orifice at which the food enters. The mouth, which lies in the right side, is called the pyloric orifice. About four inches below, in the small intestine, is another tube, which branches out (334), and, with appropriate vessels, nerves, &c., forms the largest gland in the body, called the liver, situated immediately under the diaphragm, mostly on the right side. It is divided into a large lobe, and two small ones. On the lower surface, on the right side, is the

gall bladder.   The biliary duct, after proceeding from the intestine, gives off the cistic duct to the gall-bladder.   The main duct, now the hepatic duct, divides into two tubes, one to the right and the other to the left lobe.   The nerves of the liver are principally from the hepatic plexus, formed by nerves of organic life, into which some filaments of the pneumogastric penetrate (245, 285).   By this plexus, also, the liver is brought into relation with the stomach (231).

342. The pancreas, which resembles the salivary glands in its secretion, is behind the stomach, crosswise.   It is about six inches long and one thick. Its duct enters the intestine with the biliary duct.

343. These glands are concerned in the performance of assimilation.

344. The kidneys, in the loins, are not connected with the alimentary canal. The mucous membrane continues from each kidney, and forms a long tube the size of a quill, which opens into the bladder.

346. Passing downward from the biliary and pancreatic ducts (341, 342), the intestine abounds in folds, called *valvulæ conniventes*, which increase the extent of surface, and cause its contents to descend slowly.   This intestine does not pass into the large canal as a continuous tube, but at a right angle, about four inches above its extremity, terminating in the *ileo-cœcal valve*, which extends into the large intestine, and suffers the contents of the small to pass into the large, but not those of the large into the small.   The portion of large intestine which extends below the ileo-cœcal valve is the cœcum.   It has the form of a sac opening into the colon, and is three or four inches in depth, and the same in diameter.   The colon is gathered into folds, which give it a saculated appearance, secured by three longitudinal bands.   In the rectum this form disappears, and the canal again becomes cylindrical.

347. Motion being necessary in the alimentary cavity, muscular fibres are attached to the back of the mucous membrane forming that cavity.   These are arranged according to the motion required (199).   Circular fibres surround the meatpipe, stomach, and intestines, like sections of rings, whose ends lap, to give the muscles power ; and longitudinal fibres, which run lengthwise of the meatpipe, stomach, and intestinal tube (338).   By contraction of the circular, the calibre of the cavity is diminished ; by contraction of the longitudinal fibres, the parts are shortened ; and their combined action gives a vermicular or undulating motion.   The muscular coat is more powerful in the meatpipe and stomach than in the intestine ; and in the large intestine it is thinner than in the small.   In the colon, also, the longitudinal fibres are gathered (346) into three bands.   In the rectum, the muscular coat becomes stronger, and the longitudinal fibres form a layer around the tube.   In the pharynx (338) the muscular coat is composed of six constrictor muscles, the fibres of which cross each other in various directions.   By these both the length and calibre of the pharynx are diminished.   In the stomach the fibres are disposed in three directions: longitudinally, circularly, and obliquely. At the pyloric orifice the fibres gather into a powerful ring, which, together with a folding of mucous membrane, forms the *valve of the pylorus*, or " gate-keeper."   When this is contracted the orifice is closed, so that nothing can escape from the stomach into the small intestine in a crude and undigested state.

348. The muscular coat of the alimentary organs is more or less developed according to the character of the food, which requires action in the organs, and conduces to the vigour of the muscular coat ; while the opposite conduces to emaciation. In some instances, the atrophy or wasting of the muscular coat of the stomach renders its action exceedingly feeble.

349. Such is the contractile tendency of this muscular coat, that when not distended with food the cavities are diminished, and the mucous membrane gathered into folds. In the meatpipe these are nearly longitudinal. In the stomach the wrinkles run in every direction ; but in both they disappear when distended. In the small intestine the folds are more numerous than in the stomach, and many of them permanent (346).

350. The alimentary canal is surrounded by the serous membrane which lines the thoracic and abdominal cavities (176), and constitutes one of the coats of the canal. The œsophagus is embraced by that portion which forms the partition of the chest, called the mediastinum (176), immediately in front of the spinal column. The serous membrane which surrounds the stomach and intestines, excepting the duodenum, is called their peritoneal coat. It serves (176) to isolate the organs, to present a smooth surface, which enables the organs to move without injury, and, by its attachments to the walls, to keep each portion in its proper position. The portion which secures the intestines forms a curtain from the backbone to the canal, and admits a floating motion. The curtain to the small intestine is called the mesentery, and that to the colon the mesocolon. On these curtains are distributed vessels and nerves from the alimentary canal. From the stomach, the colon, and the liver, the peritoneum depends in folds, the two sheets of which are connected by tissue containing fat. These are the omenta, or caul. The great omentum lies like an apron, floating upon the front of the small intestines. The omenta are moistened with a serous fluid ; they also receive superfluous fat. The three coats—mucous membrane, muscular coat, and peritoneal coat,—are knit together by cellular tissue. The nerves of the alimentary canal (220) are from the ganglionic system. These are abundant in the canal, imparting involuntary motion to its muscular tissue (219), giving the power of absorption, secretion, excretion, exhalation, &c., to its vessels (230) ; and sensibility (296) to its mucous membrane (290). The stomach (231) is supplied from the centre of organic life, also from the centre of animal life (245), and is thereby brought into sympathy with every part of the system (297, 298). The alimentary canal being an organ of external as well as internal relation, designed to receive nourishment for the body, and to expel the unappropriated portions, its extremities are furnished with nerves and muscles under the control of the animal centre of perception (233). The mucous membrane of the mouth, nostrils, throat, pharynx, and larynx is highly endowed with sensibility (294) ; the mouth and tongue have the sense of taste, and the nose of smell. The control of the WILL is commensurate with feeling, exercised in chewing, swallowing, speaking, singing, &c. (245—256).

351. The respiratory organs complete the process of assimilation, which commences in the stomach ; and, like the alimentary canal, the lungs, through the mucous membrane, are organs of external as well as internal relation.

352. In breathing, the windpipe, lungs, diaphragm, ribs, and breastbone are employed.

353. The mucous membrane, from the pharynx, forms the windpipe, less than an inch in diameter. This tube descends in front of the meatpipe to the chest, where it divides into two branches, to the right and left of the cavity. Here each branch divides, like an artery of a gland, into a thick brush of minute hollow twigs, each terminating in a little cell. These air cells are about the one-thousandth part of an inch in diameter, and their number in both lungs is estimated at more than one hundred millions. By this arrangement the mucous membrane of the lungs presents an extent of surface to the air equal to the whole external skin, some say greater. It has been estimated at twenty-one thousand square inches. As the air enters the windpipe and lungs principally by suction, these tubes would close if they were purely membranous. To keep them distended, therefore, and enable the respiratory apparatus to produce sound, cartilages and muscles are supplied. The parts constructed for the production of voice are at the top of the windpipe, and called the larynx, attached to the tongue, and connected with the meatpipe.

354. The larynx is composed of five cartilages, movable by several muscles. 1. The *thyroid*, or shield-like cartilage, produces at the upper part of the neck the prominence called *Adam's apple*. 2. The *cricoid*, or ring-like cartilage, is below the thyroid, and can be felt in the neck. It is narrow in front, and thick, broad, and strong behind. Its upper edge has its front fixed to the thyroid ; its lower edge is joined to the trachea. 3 and 4. The two *arytenoid*, small pyramid-shaped cartilages at the back of the larynx, above the cricoid, to which they are attached by a ligament, and upon which they have a sliding motion. 5. The *epiglottis*, a soft fibro-cartilage at the upper part of the larynx, placed over the glottis or mouth of the windpipe, which opens into the pharynx, forming a valve by which the glottis is closed in the act of deglutition (340). On the inside of the larynx are two ligaments, formed of elastic parallel fibres, extending forward from each arytenoid cartilage to the thyroid, where they meet. These are called the *chordæ vocales*, or vocal ligaments. The opening between them is the entrance into the windpipe, called the glottis. This narrow chink is capable of being enlarged, contracted, or closed. Immediately above are two small pouches, termed the ventricles of the larynx ; and above the ventricles are situated two other ligaments, extending between the arytenoid and thyroid cartilages ; so that the ventricles of the larynx are situated between these ligaments and the vocal chords.

355. The voice is produced by air passing through the larynx ; sound being occasioned by vibration of the vocal ligaments. Mayo remarks that the pitch has no reference to the aperture between the vocal chords, nor their length, but depends solely on their *tension* and the frequency of their vibrations.

356. The larynx may be elevated or depressed by muscles in the parts ; and is supplied with four nerves, furnished by the pneumogastric (245).

357. From the larynx the windpipe is kept distended by a succession of fibro-cartilaginous rings, connected by a membranous texture. These are not entire circles, but each about two-thirds of a circle, and the other third is

occupied by a texture of muscular fibres in the direction of the rings : so that their contraction draws the two ends nearer to each other, and thus diminishes the calibre of the windpipe. This portion is in the back of the windpipe, and in front of the meatpipe : so that, when food descends in the œsophagus, it is not obstructed by the rings of the windpipe, as would be the case if they continued entirely round. But if the bolus is too large, it presses in the membranous portion to such an extent as to cause choking.

358. As the branches of the windpipe become subdivided in the lungs, the rings soften down and disappear, leaving the membranous air-tubes. It is asserted by some that the muscular fibres, by the contraction of which the calibre of these tubes is diminished, are continued to the sub-divisions, and are employed in the act of expiration from the lungs (245).

359. A large artery from the heart divides into two branches, one to the right branch of the windpipe, the other to the left. These ramify, so that their branches correspond with those of the windpipe ; and, finally, the minute twigs of the artery terminate in the sides of the air-cells (353). Where the arterial capillaries terminate, the venous rise, become larger, and form branches corresponding with those of the artery, till they swell into large pulmonary veins, which emerge from the lungs and proceed to the heart.

360. These pulmonary arteries convey the blood to the lungs, where it undergoes important changes, and the veins convey it back to the heart. The lungs, however, are not nourished by this circulation. The bronchial arteries nourish the lungs, and the veins which correspond with these are ramified like those just described. Besides these, lymphatic vessels are distributed. All these vessels are supplied with nerves of organic life, which preside over their functions (230). Branches of the pneumogastric also (245), interlacing with nerves of organic life, proceed to the lungs. These are supposed by some to be appropriated to that sensibility by which we feel the want of air ; others think they are distributed to the muscles of the air-tubes (358), and convey the stimulus of motion ; others, that they perform both these offices. All these tubes, vessels, and nerves are knit into one texture by cellular tissue (171), and the whole enveloped in serous membrane (176).

361. The right lung is divided into three lobes. The left has two lobes, and is smaller than the right, to make room for the heart (171), which lies partly on the left side. Each lobe is divided into numerous lobules. The air-cells (353) of each lobule communicate, but the cells of one lobule have no communication with those of another. The two lungs are separated from each other, and the other organs, by the serous membrane, here called the pleura (176), which lines the cavity, and divides it by passing double from the breastbone to the back, thus forming a sac for each lung, and embracing the heart, large blood-vessels, and meatpipe (350), between the two sheets of the mediastinum or middle partition.

362. If the two lungs occupied one cavity, any perforation, so that the air could rush in, would arrest respiration, and death would result. But now, if one lung be disabled, the other continues to perform its function ; and life is preserved.

363. The diaphragm (175) is a membrane, attached by legs to the upper vertebræ of the loins, and arching up into the chest like a dome, being attached to the body all round, so as to divide the trunk into two large cavities (175), the thoracic and abdominal. The meatpipe, large blood-vessels, &c., pass through this partition near the spinal column. The legs and centre of the diaphragm are tendonous ; its wings muscular. By their contraction the arch is reduced to nearly a plane ; thus the cavity of the chest is enlarged and the abdomen diminished ; the liver, stomach, &c., being pressed by the descending diaphragm.

364. When the diaphragm is drawn down, and the breastbone and ribs are elevated (181), the cavity of the chest is much enlarged.

365. In breathing, the muscles which elevate the breastbone and ribs contract, whilst the diaphragm is drawn down, and thereby the chest is enlarged, and the air inflates the lungs. Then the muscles relax, and the ribs and diaphragm return to their natural position by the elasticity of the tissue (169), the force of gravity, and the pressure of other parts. By these means, and perhaps also by the contraction of the muscles of the air-tubes (358), the air is expelled from the lungs.

366. When the ribs are confined by tight clothing, the diaphragm is compelled to act alone, but respiration is much restrained. It is not by a direct action of the WILL upon the lungs, but upon the diaphragm and muscles which elevate the breastbone and ribs, and compose the larynx, that we have control over inspiration and expiration : and this (302) is necessary to protect the lungs from offensive air, and to the production of voice ; but when neither of these demands the exercise of the WILL, respiration is given. up to organic instinct, carried on without care or consciousness. The muscles of animal life, therefore, concerned in respiration, are associated with those of organic life or involuntary motion.

367. Circulation is intimately associated with respiration. The organs employed are the heart, arteries, veins, and capillary vessels (313).

368. The heart is a muscular organ (172) somewhat the shape of an inverted cone, lying between the two sheets of the pleura, which form the central partition of the chest. It is also surrounded by a sac of its own (176), called the pericardium. The heart lies partly on the middle line, and partly on the left side. It is a double organ, each half having an upper and a lower chamber The upper are called auricles, and the lower ventricles.

369. There is no communication between the two halves of the heart. The auricle on each side, however, communicates with its ventricle. The right auricle receives the dark blood that returns in the veins from all parts of the body, and, contracting, sends it into the right ventricle through an orifice furnished with folds, so arranged as to form a *triplex* valve, called the *tricuspid valve ;* which, being pressed back, closes the orifice, and prevents the blood from returning to the auricle. The pulmonary artery (359) rises from the right ventricle, and divides into branches right and left, which are ramified in the lungs. The pulmonary artery is furnished with three folds, called the

semilunar valves. These suffer the blood to pass from the heart into the artery, but prevent its returning to the heart. Through this artery the right ventricle sends its dark blood to the lungs, where it is changed into bright red arterial blood, which is conveyed to the left side of the heart by the pulmonary veins (359). These veins, advancing in two trunks, open into the left auricle. From this the blood passes into the left ventricle, through the *mitral valve,* which prevents the blood from returning to the auricle. From the left ventricle opens the great arterial trunk called the *aorta,* through which passes all the blood that nourishes the body. This is furnished with three semi-lunar valves, which suffer the blood to pass from the ventricle into the artery, but prevent its return.

372. The auricles and ventricles contract simultaneously, but alternately ; so that as the auricles contract the ventricles dilate, and *vice versa.*

373. The heart, which in its rudimental state is connected with the central brain of the nerves of organic life (219, 231), is removed as the parts are developed ; and the ganglionic masses, from which its nerves issue, are in the neck and upper part of the chest. Some branches of the pneumo-gastric (247) enter also into the cardiac plexuses, but few reach the heart. They neither bring it under the control of the WILL, nor render it cognisable to the centre of animal perception (302). The heart is independent of the WILL, yet its action is accelerated or retarded by every emotion. This depends on its sympathy with the stomach and centre of organic life, and through them with the brain (303). For the heart is in no degree the seat of those feelings which are, in common language, referred to it.

374. From the left ventricle (369) rises the great arterial trunk, the *aorta.* This ascends towards the head, and then forms an arch behind the heart, passing through the diaphragm, and dividing to proceed to the lower limbs. After leaving the heart, it gives off branches which nourish that organ ; for neither the heart nor blood-vessels receive nourishment from the blood flowing in them, but are nourished by arteries distributed for the purpose. At the top of the arch the aorta gives off three branches, divided into arteries of the head, the face and neck, the arms, &c. As the aorta descends it gives off branches to the internal organs, walls of the body, &c. These branches subdivide till they become minute twigs, lost in the parts to which they are distributed, penetrating to the smallest filaments, and dispersed so universally that it is scarcely possible to puncture any part without wounding some. These hair-sized vessels, with those of the veins, constitute the capillary system (313), in which changes in the blood are effected.

376. All vital action is attended with expenditure of power and waste of substance (192), to be replenished by the arterial blood. In the distribution of arterial vessels each organ is supplied according to its function ; and every part is so furnished that if its blood be obstructed in some vessels, it flows on in others.

377. In a limb vigorously exercised the arteries become larger, and the muscles more developed, than in one little employed, in which the size of the arteries will diminish. In case of injury to the principal artery, the smaller

arteries of the same part increase in size, and become sufficiently capacious to supply as much blood as received before.

378. Near the extremities of the arterial capillaries, those of the veins rise; and, running into others, become larger and larger, till they form a large trunk called the *vena cava*. The veins from the lower parts form the *ascending vena cava*, which opens into the right auricle of the heart. The veins from the upper part of the body form the *descending vena cava*.

379. The veins run into each other even more than the arteries; if the flow be obstructed in some it turns into others. The number of branches, compared with the trunks, is greater in the venous than in the arterial system.

380. Myriads of capillaries (287) pass through the great limiting membrane; the venous more abundant than the arterial, both in the mucous membrane and skin.

381. There is a peculiarity in the arrangement of the veins from the abdominal viscera. Those rising from the stomach, spleen, pancreas, omentum, small intestine, and colon run together (378), and form the coronary, splenic, and mesenteric veins. These, instead of advancing directly to the vena cava, unite in a large venous trunk, which plunges into the liver, where it divides in the manner of an artery, holding the same relations to the mucous membrane of the ducts that the principal artery does in other glands. This constitutes the PORTAL SYSTEM; and where these veins terminate in the biliary duct, other capillaries rise, which form the hepatic veins; and these, receiving the blood from the portal veins, and from the hepatic artery, convey it to the vena cava.

382. The portal system has an appendage called the *spleen*, in the upper back part of the abdominal cavity, between the diaphragm and left kidney. It is attached to the diaphragm, stomach, and colon by the peritoneum. The spleen is formed almost entirely of blood-vessels, lymphatics, and cells, surrounded by a sero-fibrous membrane. Its artery ramifies, and abruptly expends itself on the tissues of the organ. Its veins, *which are proportionally larger than in any other part of the body*, arise from the cells, and empty into the vena portæ; or, rather, constitute (381) part of the roots of the portal trunk (450).

383. Arteries are composed of three coats. The exterior is a dense cellular tunic. The middle coat consists of transverse circular fibre, contractile like muscular fibre. The inner is a transparent membrane, continuous with that which lines the cavities of the heart. The veins have two coats, or, more correctly, three. The outer is cellular and very strong; the middle composed of longitudinal fibres resembling the circular fibres of the arteries; the inner exceedingly thin and similar to that which lines the arteries. This coat, in the veins in which the blood ascends against gravity, is frequently folded so as to form a species of valves, which favour the course of the blood towards the heart.

384. The nerves of the blood-vessels (219, 228, 231) are from the ganglionic system.

385. In their texture the LYMPHATICS resemble the veins. They have two coats, the external, cellular, and capable of considerable extension ; the inner frequently folded, to form valves like those in the veins, giving them the appearance of being jointed. These rise from every internal and external surface of the body, so that there is scarcely a particle in the system which cannot be reached by them. Myriads rise from the skin and mucous membrane (287, 337). Many lie under the skin ; others are buried in the organs, &c.

386. At certain points the lymphatics pass through the lymphatic glands. These are small bodies varying from one-twentieth of an inch to an inch. They consist of plexuses, of lymphatics, blood-vessels, and nerves. These mostly abound in the thorax and abdomen. Leaving these, the lymphatics proceed towards the heart, and, converging from all parts, pour their contents into large veins near the bottom of the neck. Most of them terminate in the thoracic duct, which opens at the angle formed by the junction of the large vein of the head with that of the arm. The lymphatics of the right side terminate in a short tube, which opens into the corresponding vein of the right arm. Besides these many lymphatic capillaries empty into the veins in the organs, in branches of the vena portæ, &c., and veins in the lymphatic glands.

387. The lymphatic system is divided into two classes of vessels : the lymphatics proper, employed in elaborating lymph, and conveying it to the thoracic duct ; and the lacteals, employed in elaborating chyle in the alimentary cavity, conveying it also to the thoracic duct. There is no difference between a lacteal and a lymphatic vessel, except that one elaborates chyle, and the other lymph, which resembles chyle. They are assimilating organs, and though they elaborate chyle, are in fact lacteals. Chyle may be elaborated by some of these from the contents of the stomach. Experiments on animals have proved that they can be sustained for months with the pyloric orifice of the stomach (341) closed, so that the food cannot pass into the intestine ; but the process of chylification is effected by the stomach and its lacteals (471). There have also been instances of human beings who have been sustained for years in this manner, the pyloric orifice being entirely closed by disease of the parts. " Gen. Grose," says Sir Everard Home, "had no passage through the bowels for thirty years ; yet he ate heartily and was an able-bodied man. Two hours after eating he threw up the contents of his stomach remaining undisposed of." Chyle may be elaborated also from the large intestine ; nevertheless the lacteals mostly abound in the duodenùm and jejunum (338). Leaving the alimentary canal the lacteals proceed (350) towards the backbone, and having passed through the mesenteric glands, terminate in the thoracic duct (386).

389. The lymphatics may be considered an appendage to the venous system, furnishing the assimilating materials by which the body is nourished, as well as conveying the effete substances eliminated (386). The structure of the lymphatic vessels resembles that of the veins (385) into which they empty their contents.

392. The left ventricle of the heart acts with a force of six pounds on the square inch. This ventricle has about ten square inches of internal surface, consequently the force exerted in throwing the blood into the aorta is about sixty pounds. The arteries are elastic, and have the power of adapting their capacity to the quantity of blood. When animals bleed to death, and also after the heart has ceased to act in natural death, the arteries continue to diminish till all the blood is pressed out of them.

393. All vital action is attended with expenditure of power and waste of substance (376), replenished by arterial blood ; and all increased action is attended with increased flow of blood. This local increase does not depend on the heart, nor the general arteries, but the arteries of the part acting under the special centre (219) which presides over the function. Thus, when food is introduced into the stomach, the vessels become injected without any increased action of the heart and arteries. The nerves (230), perceiving the food, inform the special centre ; and, if the substance be offensive, the quantity of blood pressed into the vessels is excessive, producing congestion.

394. The heart and arteries, therefore, are concerned in the general circulation ; while the increase of blood in particular parts depends on arterial action. At every contraction of the left ventricle of the heart the aorta is dilated ; then contracts on the blood, and presses it onward through the branches (374), which act in the same manner. But both the aorta and large branches are less active in the circulation than the smaller twigs and capillary vessels.

395. The veins, as well as the capillary vessels, possess the power of propelling the fluids which circulate in them (383).

396. The sense of touch (242, 253, 287) is extended over the surface of the body ; the ends of the fingers, however, are particularly appropriated to feeling, and here most thickly cluster those tufts formed of the extremities of the nerves called papillæ (287). Touch is the primary sense, and exists in every animal (294).

397. The nerves of taste are distributed to the mouth and throat (254) ; but the papillæ in which their extremities terminate most abound in the end of the tongue.

399. The olfactory nerves (251, 252) proceed from the centre of perception (280), and terminate (287) on the surface of the nostrils and four cavities, two in the upper jaw and two in the frontal bone above the eyes, all communicating with the nostrils.

400. If the mouth and nose become dry, the senses of taste and smell are abolished. Hence the mucous membrane is *at all times* moistened and lubricated by its own exhalation (339). This is not peculiar to these parts. Throughout the mucous membrane and skin the same condition is essential to the nerves and vessels (287).

401. The senses of hearing and sight (294) minister not only to those wants which arise from the operations of the vital economy, but also to mental and moral wants. They are, therefore, of a higher order, and not susceptible of being depraved like taste and smell.

D

402. The organism appropriated to these senses is complicated, and difficult to be described. The apparatus of hearing is the most intricate piece of mechanism in the body, and little is known of its physiology.

403. According to Hayward, "The organ may be divided into the outer, inner, and middle parts, and the auditory nerve. The external ear inclines a little forwards, adapted to collect sound, which it transmits through the tube that leads to the tympanum. This tube is formed in part of cartilage, and in part bone. It has a number of glands which secrete the wax (333), and its entrance is guarded by stiff hairs.

404. "The middle part embraces the tympanum, the small bones of the ear, and the Eustachian tube (340). The membrane of the tympanum is at the bottom of the external tube. Its inner surface is covered by mucous membrane, and a nerve called the chord of the tympanum passes over it. To this is attached one of the small bones.

405. "The tympanum is a cavity between the external and internal ear. It is of cylindrical form, with openings communicating with the internal ear, and one the termination of the Eustachian tube. It also contains four little bones—the hammer, the anvil, the round bone, and the stirrup. These are connected : the end of the hammer attached to the membrane of the tympanum, and the stirrup over an opening which leads to the internal ear. Muscles are inserted into these bones, and move them in various directions. The Eustachian tube leads from the tympanum to the back of the throat (340).

406. "The internal ear is in part of the temporal bone, near the base of the skull. It is composed of three parts—the cochlea, the vestibule, and the semicircular canal. The cochlea, so called from its resemblance to a shell, is near the entrance of the Eustachian tube ; it communicates with the tympanum and the vestibule. The vestibule, in the central part of the ear, is a sort of porch which communicates, by means of the oval opening, with the tympanum, and over this opening is the stirrup. It has communications with the cochlea, the semicircular canals, and auditory tube, through which the auditory nerve passes to the ear from the brain ; and through the openings which lead from the vestibule to the tube, the branches of the nerve go to the various parts. The three semicircular canals are behind the cochlea and vestibule, and all terminate in the latter.

407. "The auditory nerve (251, 252) is divided into filaments, which pass through the minute openings, and are distributed to the semicircular canals, the cochlea, and the vestibule."

408. The membrane of the tympanum has been ruptured without impairing the hearing. All the small bones, except the stapes, have been removed by disease, and still the hearing remained. The membrane of the tympanum is, probably, designed to shut out foreign substances from the inner chambers, and thus keep the auditory nerve in the most susceptible condition ; at the same time, it is fitted to transmit vibrations.

409. "The eye is an optical instrument, of a globular form, composed of humours covered by membranes, and enclosed in several coats. These humours are—the vitreous, the crystalline, and the aqueous. The vitreous

(from its resemblance to melted glass) is in the back part, and constitutes the greater portion of the globe. It is of the consistence of the white of egg, and contained in cells formed in a membrane which covers it. On its anterior surface there is a depression, and in this is the crystalline humour, of considerable strength, having the form of a double convex lens. It is behind the pupil, and kept in its situation by a membrane called its capsule. In front of the crystalline lens is the aqueous humour, composed principally of water, with a portion of albumen. A curtain floats in the aqueous humour, attached at its circumference. This is the iris, and the opening in it is the pupil. The colour of the iris determines the colour of the eye. The back part of the iris is called the uvea. The iris divides the space between the crystalline lens and the front of the eye into the anterior and posterior chambers. The light passes through the pupil, which is dilated and contracted by the fibres of the iris according to the intensity, the power of the eye, &c.

410. "The eye has three coats. The sclerotic is a firm membrane (169), which serves to defend the eye, into which the muscles that move it in various directions are inserted. It extends over the whole except the forepart, covered by a transparent membrane. The sclerotic coat is the 'white of the eye.' Within is the choroid coat, a thin membrane, mostly of blood-vessels and nerves, attached to the sclerotic coat, and of the same extent. On the inner surface of the choroid is the black pigment, of great importance in the function of vision.

411. "The inner coat, if not an expansion of the optic nerve, is composed of nervous filaments, called the retina (252), surrounding the globe, except the opening in front, to the edge of which the iris is attached by the ciliary ligament, and over which is placed the convex transparent membrane called the cornea.

412. "The optic nerves (251, 252) do not enter the eyeballs in the centre, but a short distance towards the nose. The eyelids have a thin skin on the outside, muscular fibres beneath, and a cartilage on their edges. They are lined by a mucous membrane, which is the tunic which connects the eyeballs with the lids. It is loosely attached to the eyelids, so as to allow free motion."

413. The fluid which continually moistens the eye is secreted by the lachrymal gland (334, 345) within the orbit, at the outer angle. The fluid thus secreted passes through two small openings, and is thence conveyed into the nose by the nasal duct. These canals, from inflammation, may be obstructed, and then the moisture accumulates till it flows over the lid. When the lachrymal glands are excited by irritations or emotions, they pour their fluid into the eyes more rapidly than the ducts can convey it, and it overflows the eyelids upon the cheeks.

414. Each eye has six muscles, which turn it in every direction. These are among the most curious parts of the visual apparatus. Nerves convey the stimulus of motion to these muscles (248, 249). Those which impart feeling to the eyes, ears, nose, and mouth are from the trifacial.

416. Light is the medium of vision. Take a glass of considerable magnifying power, cut a hole in a shutter to receive it, close the shutter, and exclude all light except what passes through the glass; then, if the sun is shining, the rays will pass from the glass and converge till they meet in a focus, and then diverge beyond; the diverging forming the same angle at the focal point as the converging rays. At this point the rays cross, so that the top ones at the glass are at the bottom beyond the point, and *vice versâ*. If a sheet of white paper be placed a little beyond the focal point, a miniature image will appear of whatever the rays may come from which pass through the glass, and have the colours of the objects reflected; but the image will be upside down, caused by the crossing of the rays. The rays cross by passing through the glass, which is thicker in the centre than at the circumference, and—being more dense than the atmosphere—bending the rays towards each other as they pass. The rays will bend more or less in passing as the glass is more or less convex: the more convex, the sooner will the rays cross. If a glass globe filled with water be placed in the hole, the rays will cross before they get through, and the image will be thrown upon the back of the globe.

417. This is a description of a *camera obscura*, the best illustration of the eye. The interior of the eye is the darkened room; the cornea, the transparent glass; the iris, the shutter; the pupil, the hole through which the rays enter; and the aqueous, crystalline, and vitreous humours constitute a lens of so great a convexity, that the rays cross and diverge before they get through the globe, and throw their inverted image upon the retina, where the mind perceives the image, which the judgment contrives to get right end upwards.

418. Sometimes, from the shape of the eye-ball, or the crystalline lens, the rays of light cross too near the cornea (411), and the image upon the retina is indistinct. This is the case with near-sighted people. When the eye becomes enfeebled, from the falling back of the lens or the flattening of the ball, the focal point is formed too near the retina, and the image rendered imperfect. In the former case spectacles with concave, and in the latter with convex, glasses assist the eye in forming its focus at the proper distance from the retina; the concave glasses, by spreading out the rays, and thus preventing their crossing so soon; and the convex, by bringing the rays nearer before they enter the eye, and causing them to cross sooner. *Physiological powers, however, are always impaired by artificial means;* and, though it may be convenient to have recourse to glasses to regulate the focal distance of the eye, thousands of eyes are thus injured where one is benefited.

420. Every hair has, under the skin, its root—a small oval pulp, invested by a sheath, and supplied with vessels. The shaft above the surface consists of a horny substance resembling the epidermis (287).

421. The health of the hair depends on the root. Every injury to the digestive organs, and every violent excitement of the mind, affects the hair. Violent grief has covered many a head with grey hairs, and paroxysms of fear have produced the same effect in a few hours; but dietetic errors are the general causes of baldness in civic life. When the colouring matter ceases to be deposited, the hair becomes white. All applications, except in so far as

they contribute to the vigour of the roots by cleanliness, are useless and injurious. In a healthy state the hair is supplied with an oily secretion, and can never be benefited by any other unction.

422. The nails are pliable or brittle according to the general health, and are destroyed by disease, or by the medicinal substances employed to cure disease.

VIII.

426. The saliva is *a solvent fluid*, and when mastication is properly performed, digestion commences in the mouth. By imperfect mastication a fourfold injury is done. It compels the stomach to receive the food too rapidly (429) ; to secrete a larger quantity of solvent fluid than would be necessary if the functions of the mouth had been properly performed ; to reduce by maceration those masses which ought to have been broken down by the teeth ; and by increasing the expenditure of functional power, causes a greater degree of vital exhaustion of the stomach, tending to debility and disease.

428. As soon as the œsophagus receives the food, it contracts (338, 347), and presses it onward into the stomach.

429. When food reaches the stomach, little *feelers* (230, 287, 290) inform the presiding centre (220), which throws its stimulus on the tissues (313) ; the muscular fibres (347) are called into action ; an increase of arterial blood is injected (393) ; the nervous power (164) exalted, and the temperature elevated. The muscular fibres throw the stomach into a gentle commotion, by which the food is carried round, and pressed against the internal surface. This excites the glands (332) that secrete a fluid, which begins to exude in small drops, and mingle with the food. This is the *gastric juice;* from the Greek *gaster*—stomach. After the food has been mixed with this fluid, if the stomach be not embarrassed by too rapid swallowing, its muscles relax to prepare for another portion, which, when received, undergoes the same process. These operations continue till the meal is finished, when the muscular action becomes less rapid, and a vermicular motion is kept up till the function of the stomach is completed, and its contents emptied into the intestine.

431. The gastric juice is the principal agent of the change which the food undergoes in the stomach. This fluid, as well as that secreted by the salivary glands and the pancreas, has been analysed by chemists without advantage to physiology or medicine. As a matter of chemical science, we know what substances are obtained by analysis of the fluid taken from the stomach, but not the least ray of light is thereby thrown upon physiology. We know no better what are the properties of this fluid in the living stomach by which it produces specific effects in the vital process of digestion ; and should we attempt to assist the stomach by any of those substances which result from analysis of the gastric juice, we should be more likely to injure than to benefit the organ. Both the chemical and physiological character of the gastric juice is affected by dietetic habits, the general state of the health, affections of the mind, and

conditions of the stomach.   This is also true of the salivary, pancreatic, and
all the fluids of the body.   Theories founded on chemical knowledge in regard
to the assimilating changes produced by the organic economy are established
in utter darkness, and more frequently the source of evil than good.

432. Gastric juice can be taken from the stomach and put upon food in a
glass vessel, and, if kept at the temperature of the stomach (434), it will digest
the food.   Even an artificial gastric juice will digest the food as well as the
fluid taken from the stomach.   But neither the artificial nor real gastric juice
can effect the changes in an inorganic vase which are produced in the living
stomach.   They may *macerate* the substances, and reduce them to the *consistency* and *appearance* of the digested contents of the stomach, but they
cannot produce genuine chyme, from which the organs of the body can
elaborate chyle.

433. The gastric fluid is, in truth, a vital solvent ; for it is only when acting
under the vital control of the living organ that it can be the agent of that vital
change essential to chymification.   Even in the stomach, when digestion is
going on, if the nervous power be diminished (164), the process will be retarded,
or arrested, whilst inorganic affinities become active, and inorganic combinations result, in direct hostility to the vital welfare.   Not only disintegration
and decomposition, but new combinations take place in the vital changes
which are effected by the digestive organs ; these (117) are the results of forces
which act in opposition to the inorganic affinities, which are subdued, and the
vital affinities superinduced, only by the influence of the living organ (121.)

434. During the early stages of digestion, the pyloric orifice of the stomach
(341) is closed by the pylorus (347), so that the contents cannot be pressed
into the intestine by the action of the stomach, but the mass is kept in motion,
and becomes permeated by the gastric juice.   The temperature of the stomach
is somewhat elevated by the concentration of vital power.   In a healthy body
it varies from a hundred, to a hundred and four, *Fahrenheit.*   When the
digestive organs have been impaired, and chronic irritability induced, this
vital energy during digestion is often attended with a disagreeable chilliness
of the external surface, and symptoms of fever, especially if the dietetic habits
are objectionable.

435. By the gastric juice, the food is reduced to a pultaceous mass, in a
proximate state of chymification.   The portions in contact with the mucous
membrane are then acted on by the vital powers of the stomach, and the
nutritious properties converted into a substance different from anything in
the food when received.   This is real chyme—said to be homogeneous—and
so far as chemical tests can determine, it is nearly identical in character, whatever be the food from which it is formed.   But in regard to physiological
qualities, its character varies with the food (456.)

436. When the portion in contact with the mucous membrane is converted
into chyme, it is carried by muscular action of the stomach towards the pylorus
(347), which opens, and suffers it to pass into the intestine (338).   When in a
healthy state, if undigested food attempts to pass with the chyme, the pylorus
closes, and the intruder is carried back, to be subjected to the operations of the

stomach. If it be indigestible, it is finally either permitted to pass into the intestine, or ejected through the mouth. But when the stomach is debilitated (296), the integrity of the pylorus is impaired, and crude substances are permitted to pass into the intestine, where they become causes of irritation, producing disturbance and fatal disorder.

437. When one portion is chymified and removed into the duodenum, another comes in contact with the surface of the stomach, and is operated on in the same manner, till the whole is chymified and carried into the intestine. But if the chymified portion is not removed, the process is arrested. It is therefore essential that every portion should come in contact; hence muscular action is as essential to the function of the stomach as nervous.

438. All substances suitable for food consist of certain proportions of nutritious and innutritious matter, and the alimentary organs are constituted to act upon such substances. Therefore, it is only the nutritious portion of the matter that is converted into chyme. The innutritious portion is separated from the nutritious, and reduced to a state fit to pass along the alimentary tube as fecal matter. Nor is it true that all the nutritious properties of our food are chymified in the stomach, for this process (320) is common to the whole alimentary cavity. In the gastric cavity a general solution of the matter is effected, and the assimilating change far advanced. In some parts, indeed, chymification is perfected for the action of the organs which elaborate chyle; and this matter is acted on to some extent by those organs before it leaves the stomach (388). In other portions of the nutritious matter the chymifying change is not perfected in the gastric cavity, the process remaining to be completed in the alimentary canal.

439. Some kinds of food pass through the stomach more slowly than others: the stomach of one individual differs from another in regard to the time employed; and the same stomach varies in this respect with varying circumstances; but, as a general statement, the food received undergoes digestion, and passes from the stomach into the duodenum, in from two to five hours.

440* Water does not appear to undergo any change in the gastric cavity, but is removed by absorption in a very few minutes, if the stomach is healthy, and still more rapidly, when the mucous membrane (338) is inflamed, under symptoms of fever, with great thirst. In chronic dyspepsia, absorption often takes place slowly, and water will remain for hours, retarding digestion, causing acidity, flatulence, and eructations; and, perhaps, will be thrown up, with undigested food. When water, holding in solution any nutritious matter, as broth or soup, is taken, the aqueous part is absorbed before digestion commences. Milk is managed in a similar manner. The gastric juice separates the curd from the aqueous portion; the latter is absorbed, and the curd digested. But indigestible substances in aqueous solution are absorbed with the water, and pass into the vital domain with no apparent change.

441. There is on every surface a vasculo-nervous web formed by the minute extremities of arteries, veins, lymphatics, and nerves (287). Of these vessels, the veins appear the more numerous. On the question whether the lymphatics absorb both assimilated and unassimilated substances, or only assimilated, and

* In the original American edition this paragraph, 440, was erroneously numbered 450, and so on to the end of the work. Mr. Dombusch having corrected this error, and made his index to correspond, his arrangement has been adopted here.—ED.

the veins only unassimilated substances, some have embraced one view, and some the other. Undoubtedly, both the venous capillaries and lymphatics *can* be made to absorb foreign substances, but the fact settles no principle in physiology. The question is not, what are the abnormal possibities ? but what are the regular functions of the parts in the normal condition of the vital economy ? There is little reason to doubt that, in the regular performance of their functions, the lymphatics, including the lacteals (387), are confined to assimilated substances, and foreign substances are absorbed by the venous capillaries. It is, however, probable, that foreign substances find their way into the lymphatic extremities which inosculate with the venous capillaries, and which transfer those substances to the veins in the lymphatic glands, in the portal system, and other points (386).

442. The venous capillaries, then, absorb the water and other substances that pass unchanged into the vital domain ; and these capillaries are the radicals of the great venous trunk (381), through which unassimilated substances that enter the circulation find their way to the vena cava (378).

443. The pyloric being nearly on a level with the cardiac orifice of the stomach (341), its contents do not descend into the intestine, but are pressed through by the muscular fibres (347). But there is little of this action when water is received, consequently little passes into the intestine, but is taken up by the absorbents. When deleterious substances are mingled with water, however, the absorbents receive it reluctantly ; and, as the stomach will not long retain it, a considerable portion is expelled into the intestine. Hence, when ardent spirit is given to animals, which are shortly after killed and examined, the mucous membrane, not only of the stomach, but also of the intestine, is found highly inflamed.

444. The integrity of the digestive function, then, depends on vigorous nervous power (164), healthy secretion (429), and muscular action (347) ; neither of which can be impaired without injuring the others. The nervous power suffers from inordinate mental excitement, especially the depressing passions (304). Narcotic, and all purely stimulating substances, also impair the nervous power. Improper food, gluttony, everything that tends to impair health, serves to diminish this power, and these causes affect the secretions and muscular action of the stomach.

445. As the chyme passes into the intestine (338), it is perceived by nerves in the mucous membrane (287, 290), and muscles are excited, causing a worm-like motion, by the successive contraction of the fibres (347). By this the chyme is carried along the intestinal tube, its course been retarded by the semilunar folds of the membrane ; and a solvent fluid, resembling the gastric juice, exudes from the vessels (339).

446. When the chyme enters, the lacteals (388) begin to elaborate from it their peculiar fluid—the chyle (153). As the chyme moves along, the chymifying process is carried on by the vital secretions of the tube ; so that, while the lacteals in one part are acting on the assimilated portion, the less perfectly assimilated is preparing for the lacteals of the succeeding part. In this manner the two processes are carried on until all the nutritious matter is

converted into chyme and chyle. Some suppose these processes are continued in the large intestine, and that the cæcum (346) acts as a kind of second stomach, to complete digestion. The principal office of the large intestine, however, is to dispose of the fecal matter of the food. The perfect performance of the functions of the intestine requires that the stomach should not be employed at the same time ; hence, the reception of food at improper times, and all dietetic irregularities, always disturb the functions of the intestine.

447. The pancreas (342) is like the salivary glands. There is no difference between the salivary, gastric, and pancreatic fluids ; the different degrees of acid, &c., found in one or the other of these being accidental, and owing to the physiological condition of the system, or state of particular organs. The pancreatic fluid is employed in perfecting chymification in the intestine ; accordingly the pancreas, as well as the salivary glands, is largest in animals which subsist on food that requires the greatest quantity of solvent fluid for its chymification.

448. To understand the use of the bile, it is necessary to survey most of the abdomen. 1. The alimentary canal presents a surface of about thirteen square feet, everywhere covered by minute vessels, employed in the performance of important functions (331), the venous capillaries being the most numerous. 2. These venous capillaries, together with those of the spleen (381), the pancreas, the mesenteric glands, &c. (386), run into veins, which unite to form the great venous trunk of the portal system (381). 3. This portal trunk (378) plunges into the liver (335, 341), where it is ramified like an artery, holding the same relation to the biliary ducts that arteries do to the ducts of other glands (334), and forming the greatest part of the substance of the organ ; while the hepatic artery is designed for the nourishment of the liver. The finest ramifications of this artery, however, also enter the vena portæ ; and the hepatic veins receive their blood, not from the artery, but from the vena portæ. 4. A quantity of arterial blood is sent to the stomach and intestine during digestion ; and a large proportion of this, remaining after the tissues are nourished (376), is, by these processes, converted into venous blood, and must be returned to the heart for renovation. 5. Many substances are absorbed, unchanged, and mingled with the venous blood just spoken of ; hence this blood, so freighted with impurities, instead of returning to the heart in the manner of venous blood from other parts, is furnished with vessels which constitute the portal system (381), by which it is poured into the largest gland of the body. Thus the venous blood from the alimentary canal, with all its foreign impurities, is filtered through the liver before it returns to the general circulation ; and the liver secretes the bile from the blood thus furnished by the portal veins, and not from arterial blood ; the latter being necessary only to nourish the tissues of the organ ; after having done which, and become venous blood, it enters with the portal blood into the venous plexus where the bile is secreted. Therefore, in the absence of supplies from the vena portæ, bile *can* be secreted from the blood which enters the liver by the hepatic artery. When foreign substances are absorbed, if detected, they are found in the blood of the spleen, the portal veins, and the liver, when no

trace of them appears in the thoracic duct (386) nor the general circulation. Indeed, there is a way by the intercommunication of the veins and lymphatics (386) through which unassimilated substances are carried off to the kidneys, lungs, skin, &c., without being permitted to enter the general circulation. But when deleterious substances are habitually received, the organic sensibility (296) is gradually depraved, and functional integrity impaired, till those substances pass into the circulation. And hence when ardent spirit is occasionally drunk, it can rarely be detected in the general circulation, even when exhaled from the lungs ; but when an habitual drunkard continues his inebriation for days, the blood taken from the arm is found charged with alcohol.

449. The bile is not concerned in the formation of chyle further than it may assist in solution, preparatory to chymification ; for both chyme and chyle are produced without any agency of the bile (388). The liver is developed, and performs its function before chymification and chylification take place. If the liver had been designed to secrete a fluid essential to the assimilating processes, it would be furnished with no reservoir to retain its secretion, but would secrete its fluid only when required, and pour it where needed. But the secretion is continually going on ; and because the bile cannot be continually poured into the intestine, consistently with the regulations of the vital economy, the liver is furnished with a reservoir (341), which retains it until an opportunity is afforded for its discharge.

450. The venous blood of the portal system is a large quantity, and the whole must filtrate through the liver (448), before it reaches the heart ; furthermore, the quantity is not always the same. The arterial supply being increased during digestion (393), there is a commensurate increase of the venous blood. At the same time, aqueous fluid may be absorbed (440), and mingled with this blood in the portal veins, suddenly increasing its volume. It follows either that this fluid is driven through the liver with rapidity, or that the veins are suddenly distended, or that there is a vascular appendage as a reservoir to receive a portion and retain it till the liver is prepared to act upon it. Precisely such is found in the spleen (382). The structure of that organ, its connection with the portal system, the increase of its volume with the increase of venous blood, its enlargement when fluids are absorbed, and the fact that foreign substances are found in its blood—the fact also that it can be extirpated from the body without destroying life—concur to prove that the spleen is a reservoir to the portal system ; the whole constituting an apparatus to receive the venous blood, mingled with whatever foreign substances may be absorbed, and so purify that blood as to prepare it to return to the heart. Nor does this purification consist exclusively in the secretion of bile, but the apparatus has communication with the kidneys, lungs, &c., through which it disposes of unassimilated substances (448).

451. The function of the liver, therefore, is that of a cleansing organ ; and the bile is *primarily* an excrementitious substance, carried off with the fecal matter ; hence it enters the small intestine when it is distended, and mixes with the fecal matter. It is true, that though the bile is secreted for

the primary purpose of purifying the blood, and is an excrementitious substance, yet it is made subservient to the chymifying process.

452. Nearly all the substances on which man subsists contain oily matter ; and the gastric juice has little effect on it until changed by other means. When lean flesh, or vegetable substances best adapted to the wants of man, are received into the stomach, the oily matter is in so small a proportion, and so diffused, that the food is sufficiently digested to afford chyme for the action of the lacteals, and fit it to enter the duodenum with little change.   Soon after, the bile is mixed with it (341), acting on the oily matter as an alkali, and converting it into a saponaceous substance, which is, by the solvent fluid from the pancreas, &c. (445, 447), converted into chyme.   But when a considerable proportion of the food consists of animal fat, or vegetable oil, it cannot be so far chymified in the stomach as to fit it to enter the intestine without disturbance.   The stomach is irritated by the unmanageable substance, and the biliary apparatus sympathising (297, 341), pours the bile into the duodenum, where, instead of descending in the usual manner (341), it is carried up, and admitted to assist the stomach by converting the oily matter into a kind of soap, soluble by the gastric juice.   But this introduction of the bile into the stomach is incompatible with the best functional integrity of that organ.

453. Besides the oily matter, there is more acid in some food than is consistent with the welfare of the intestines ; and this may be neutralised by the alkaline properties of the bile in the duodenum.

454. To act as an alkali on the oil and acids in the intestines is the *secondary* important use of the bile, in no other manner concerned in the production of chyle.

455. The chyle (447) has been supposed to be formed in the intestine and to be sucked up by the lacteals ; hence these vessels are said to *absorb* the chyle.   But there is no chyle formed in the cavity, and the function of the lacteals is rather that of *secretion* than absorption, for they elaborate a new substance from the chymified food, and in this process there is a further decomposition of the matter, and new combinations, so that the chyle possesses a nature essentially different from the chyme (140).   This is a vital function which has foiled the ingenuity of chemists, who, taking the analysis of dead matter for their data (147), have endeavoured to reason out the laws of organic combination.   In vain have they attempted to regulate diet on chemical principles (151), and insisted on the necessity for certain properties to sustain the vital economy.   That economy triumphs over the affinities and laws of inorganic matter, and bends them to its purposes, transmuting from one form to another the substances which science calls elements (51), and elaborating from every aliment a chyle so identical in its *chemical* character, that chemists can scarcely detect the least appreciable difference.*

456. The lacteals possess the transmuting power of vitality in an eminent

---

* The world has been greatly misled on this subject. We have been told that chyle from vegetable, contains much more carbon and less nitrogen than that from animal food ; but all such statements are incorrect. The chyle formed from vegetable and from animal matter are identical in chemical composition.

degree. The chyle nearest the secreting mouths is of a different nature from the chyme (153). It is a thin fluid, of a milky appearance, slightly albuminous, and contains the globules (157) peculiar to animalised matter, which are supposed to be the nuclei of all the solids in the body. The colour varies, being more white in proportion as oily matter abounds. As the chyle passes through the mesenteric glands (386) it is more assimilated, and, before it mingles with the blood, is like it in all respects, excepting colour (154). The proportion of globules to its other properties is so nearly the same when the food is either exclusively vegetable or animal, that the difference is scarcely appreciable. But the chyle from vegetable food differs in one respect from that formed from animal food. When taken from its living organs, the chyle elaborated from animal food putrefies in three or four days, while that from vegetable food may be kept several weeks without becoming putrid. This is an important fact, not appreciated by physiologists (914).

457. The mesenteric glands are (386) plexuses of vessels and nerves, having none of the characteristics of secreting organs, and more properly called vascular ganglions. These consist of lacteals or lymphatics, with which are associated veins arising from the ganglions, and which communicate with the lacteals. These ganglions establish such communications between the lacteals and the veins as enable the former to expel foreign substances which cannot safely pass into the thoracic duct.

459. When the chyle reaches the thoracic duct (386), into which it is conveyed by the lacteals, it is possessed of considerable intrinsic vitality (203), and abounding in animal molecules (456). Before leaving the thoracic duct, each of these molecules becomes surrounded by a thin tunic, and thus prepared to enter the circulation, and to become the globules of the blood. The chyle is carried up by the thoracic duct, and emptied into the subclavian vein from the left arm (386).

461. The blood diffused for the nourishment of the system is not all appropriated in its first distribution, but a considerable proportion is returned to the heart (368, 369). In consequence, however, both of the absence of properties abstracted by the arterial capillaries, and the presence of others accumulated in the circulation, the venous blood returns full of impurities, and unfitted to supply the wants of the system.

462. But while passing through the lungs, the chyle and venous blood undergo those changes by which they both become arterial blood.

468. As cleansing organs the lungs eliminate the impurities of the blood, in a manner corresponding with the functions of the skin (289) ; and as organs of nutrition they digest the air, and convert a portion of it into the substance of the blood.

469. As depurating organs, they excrete from the venous blood substances, the elimination of which is necessary. As soon as the excreted substances are thrown into the air-cells (353), the matter issues from the lungs in the form of vapor, carbonic acid gas, etc. The vapor thus thrown from the lungs sometimes amounts to nearly a quart of water in twenty-four hours. A portion of this is supposed to come from the chyle. The quantity of carbonic

acid gas discharged is also considerable. This gas is unfit for respiration, and when inhaled without a mixture of air, it causes suffocation. This effect, however, is owing to the absence of oxygen; for carbonic acid gas can be introduced into the stomach without any of the effects of poison. By the consumption of the oxygen, and the generation of this gas by burning charcoal, life is often destroyed; and for the same reason, a number of people in a close room, by respiration, render the air impure. Were it not for a benevolent arrangement in regard to this gas, all animals would soon be destroyed (143). Being heavier than air, it sinks below the nostrils during the pause which follows expiration, and thus is prevented from being drawn into the lungs in the succeeding inspiration. Descending, it becomes diffused, and is taken up by vegetables, and the carbon retained (143.)

470. When the blood in the lungs is purified, it is prepared to receive assimilated air. This is a vital process. The lungs are constantly receiving fresh supplies (438), and although expiration follows inspiration, the lungs are never exhausted, but a volume of air remains in them five times larger than that which is inhaled at an ordinary inspiration. The air which we expire, is little, if any of that which was received by the immediately preceding inspiration, and thus an aerial circulation takes place.

472. Oxygen is the nutrient property of the air (465), and hence is said to support respiration (92); yet it never becomes incorporated with the blood *as oxygen* (112), but in the vital process is converted into the substance of the blood; and then it is not oxygen but blood. Nor is it till vitality is destroyed, and its nature changed, that oxygen can be obtained from blood. The quantity of oxygen consumed by an individual is said to vary with the exercise, state of mind, health, food, temperature, etc. More is consumed when the weather is cold than warm, and more during digestion, but less is consumed when the food is vegetable than animal, less when the body is at rest, and the mind calm. The average quantity is about two pounds and eight ounces, troy, per day.

476. The blood in an ordinary-sized man, is from three to four gallons. Of this, about one-fourth is contained in the arteries, and two-thirds in the veins (379), a large proportion in the capillary vessels (313). The ventricles of the heart contract from seventy to seventy-five times in a minute; and the left ventricle throws into the aorta from one to two ounces of blood at every contraction, so that the whole volume of blood passes through the heart once in three minutes. In a new-born infant the heart contracts about one hundred and forty times in a minute; in the first year one hundred and twenty-four times; and in the second, one hundred and ten, and in the third, ninety-six times. In the decline of life, the pulse does not exceed sixty in a minute. The rapidity varies according to circumstances. In some the heart contracts more than four thousand times in an hour; in others, less than three thousand. This difference (909) depends much on dietetic and other habits.

478. The blood is a living fluid (203), and its vitality is susceptible of considerable increase and diminution; still, its vitality cannot be sustained out of the living vessel more than a few minutes; but if blood be confined to a

living artery, its vitality will be preserved as long as the healthy vitality of the artery remains. The preservation of the blood, therefore, depends on the vessels, or rather on the nerves of organic life which preside over their functions (219), and the degree of vitality varies with the condition of these nerves, whilst the condition of the nerves depends much on the character of the blood.

479. If the blood in the system be excessive, there is a tendency to congestion, inflammation, and death. If too far reduced, the energy of the nervous system is diminished, the power of the blood vessels is impaired, and the vitality of the blood lessened.

482. When taken from the living body and permitted to stand a short time, a portion of it gathers into a thick clot, and the remainder is a thin, transparent fluid of a greenish or yellowish appearance, called serum. By washing the clot, it becomes white and has a fibrous appearance. When putrefaction commences in blood, it attacks rather the coagulum than the serous portion, and this is true also of the chyle.

483. This is as far as the *physiologist* can push his analysis; and *this* justifies the conclusion that the blood is not a homogeneous fluid, but consists of globules held in a fluid state by an aqueous diluent, and that its vitality resides in the globules.

484. All the absorbent vessels pour their contents, whether salutary or deleterious, into the veins. (440) Water, holding saline substances, may be injected without destroying life. Medicinal substances may be introduced in the same manner; and poisonous substances pass unchanged (448). Alcohol is sometimes present in the blood in so concentrated a form, as to burn with a blue flame. When death is caused by lightning, the blood remains fluid; and in putrid fever, also, the corpuscles lose the power of coagulating (482).

485. These facts prove that the serum of the blood cannot possess vitality; and leave little room to doubt, that the colouring matter which surrounds the globules (481), *is intended to shield them from the pernicious influences of such foreign matter as may become mixed with the serum.* While the corpuscles remain in the lacteals, where only assimilated fluids enter, they are not invested with those pellicles which become red in the lungs (459); and when they enter into the arrangements of organised structure, they are again divested of those tunics; hence, they are only thus covered while in the circulation, exposed to the influence of unassimilated substances.

486. It is possible that impurities in the blood exert their deleterious influence first on the nervous tissue (230), and nerves of organic life, producing irritation, thus communicated to the globules of the blood, producing fever. Hence, the thirst which attends fever, and which may be a demand for water to displace the offensive serum and allay the preternatural heat. Hence, also, the fact, that water is the most efficient febrifuge. Violent fevers have been subdued by it with rapidity, when medical practice had proved ineffectual.

487. The temperature of the blood (129) is ordinarily 98 degrees *Fah.*, being about the same upon the polar seas or under the line.

488. The vital properties which constitute the functional powers of the

organs are rapidly exhausted by action, and replenished by the fresh arterial blood (376). This being withheld, the muscles lose their susceptibility and contractility ; the sensorial power of the nerves is suspended, and the nervous power is lost (461). The blood cannot be fitted for the replenishment of the system, without respiration, and oxygen is essential to this function (472). In this view oxygen is essential to the production of animal heat, but not as a chemical element (139).

489. Animal heat is a result of vital function, depending on the nerves of organic life (228). Whatever impairs the health of the nerves, diminishes the power of the body to regulate its temperature. Hence, spirit-drinkers, except under the influence of the stimulus, have less power to resist cold, in proportion as their nervous system has been impaired. Indigestion, and other difficulties of the stomach, connected with the nerves diminish the powers of reaction.

490. The relaxing effects of heat, diminish the power to sustain cold. They also diminish the powers of digestion, and render the system more susceptible of injury from dietetic irregularities. On the other hand, except in disease, cold weather, if not too intense, invigorates the body, increasing its ability to generate heat and the powers of digestion ; but sudden and extreme cold depresses the system.

491. Heat (129) radiates from the body as from inorganic bodies ; hence, the temperature is lower near the surface than in the central parts ; but this by no means sustains the conjecture that the calorific function is peculiar to the internal parts.

493. Blood being distributed to every part (475) is appropriated, and every structure is furnished with supplies of its proper substance. The bones, cartilages, ligaments, tendons, membranes, muscles, and nerves, all receive new homogeneous matter, elaborated by the vital processes from the same current. How these processes of assimilation are effected is unknown. Conjectures advanced have ended in guessing. Not a trace of gelatin has ever been found in the blood, although this substance enters more into the solid forms of matter than any other. Some suppose that the capillary extremities secrete the substance of each structure, but with the microscope, they are unable to detect any difference between the vessels which secrete these substances. Even those which supply the teeth and the brain appear alike ; yet the substances secreted are as unlike as any two in nature.

494. All the changes are effected by vital chemistry, which decomposes the simplest forms of matter (139), by laws peculiar to vitality, in opposition to the affinities of inorganic chemistry (121—123).

495. If a bone be broken, or muscle or nerve wounded, the vital economy immediately sets about healing the breach. The blood coagulates in the breach, for the double purpose of staunching the wound, and forming a matrix for regeneration of the parts. Minute vessels shoot out into the coagulum, and deposite bony matter where it is required to unite a fractured bone, and nervous substance to heal the wounded nerve, etc. But the vital economy seems not to possess the power of reproducing true muscle (201), therefore,

when any fleshy part has been wounded, its breach is repaired by a gelatinous substance which becomes hard, sometimes assuming a fibrous appearance, and perfectly unites the divided muscles.

497. The blood from which the solids are elaborated, is also the source from which the different vessels (313), follicles (333), and glands (334) exhale or secrete (330) the fluid which perspires from the skin, and mucous membrane (339) of the lungs, nose, ears, eyes, etc.; that which exhales from the serous membrane of the closed cavities (178), lubricates the heart (368), thorax, and abdomen (175); moistens the brain (272) and spinal marrow; the joints (185), tendons, etc. (195); the serous fluid of the cellular tissue (171); and the adipose matter (178) of the same (498); the marrow of the bones (179); the humors of the eye (409); the wax of the ears (333); tears (413), saliva (340), gastric juice (332), pancreatic fluid (447), bile (451), etc. How these secretions are effected, we know as little as how the solid structures are produced. The vital forces possess a transmuting power (62), as they elaborate from a few kinds of food and the air, all the different substances, with properties so diversified, and which afford many substances which cannot be accounted for from anything contained in the blood, or any known principles of chemical combination.

498. Fat is contained in cells, which vary in size, and do not communicate. It is *always* found in the cellular tissue of the orbits of the eyes, the soles of the feet, the pulp of the fingers and toes; and sometimes in great abundance in the cellular tissue under the skin, and which surrounds the heart, kidneys, etc.; while in the eyelids, the brain, the eyes, ears, nose, lungs, intestinal canal, glands, and other parts, it is *never* found, except as the effect of disease. The quantity of fat in the body varies greatly (178). Sometimes it constitutes a considerable proportion of the body. In the orbits of the eyes, the soles of the feet, etc., it serves the purpose of the elastic cushions, giving facility to movements, diminishing the effect of pressure, etc. Under the skin, it is supposed, as a non-conductor, to assist in preserving the temperature from the effects of cold; and it is a prevailing opinion that this matter is a provision against famine. But if the fat be designed for nourishment during protracted fasts, etc., then if a very fat man and a lean one be shut up to die of starvation, the fat man ought to diminish in weight more slowly, and to live longer than the lean man, but the contrary of this is true. The lean man will lose weight much more slowly, and live several days longer than the fat one.

499. If from excessive alimentation, want of exercise, or any other cause, nutrition becomes excessive, disease must result, without some mode of relief. More nutritious matter is received than the wants of the vital economy demand. None of the structures can incorporate it, and it cannot be eliminated. In this exigency it must be disposed of in the safest manner possible, as a temporary resource. The cellular tissue (158) is the lowest structure in vital endowment. In the cells of this tissue, employed as a kind of web to connect other parts (171), the vital economy may deposit substances which it is not able to eliminate. Some thus deposited, and retained for years, are of the most deleterious character (1265).

500. It is a general law, that when decomposition exceeds nutrition, the absorbents first remove those substances which are of least use, hence all morbid accumulations, as wens, tumors, abscesses, etc., are diminished and often removed under protracted fasting. When adipose matter has been deposited also, if exercise be increased, or food diminished, the eliminating organs, by all that their functions are relatively increased upon nutrition, will remove the adipose matter to restore health.

501. The accumulation of fat evinces diseased action in some of the organs, and can only be carried to a limited extent without terminating either in morbid obesity, dropsy, or apoplexy, or reacting on some of the organs of the digestive apparatus. Hence, almost every animal fatted for human food, is in a state of disease when butchered. It is difficult to find in the markets of our cities a perfectly healthy liver from a fatted animal; and it is by no means an uncommon thing for hogs to die of disease when about to be killed.

503. Decomposition is effected by the lymphatics (387, 388) which (385) arise from every portion of the body; and they are acting on every substance where nutrition is performed, decomposing to a fluid lymph, the hardest bones as well as the softest structures. Thus, by the constant operations of the nutritive organs, and the lymphatics, every structure in the body is continually undergoing composition and decomposition, renovation and decay (314, 499). Particle by particle of new matter is added from the blood, and particle by particle of old matter is absorbed and converted to lymph. So that while the constitution of every structure remains permanent, a continual change is taking place in the matter of which our bodies are composed; completed as often as once in seven years (314).

505. The lymphatics possess an assimilating power (441), by which they convert many of the substances they absorb into a homogeneous fluid, which mingles with the chyle, and passes into the blood-vessels (476). And when supplies of food are small, the lymphatics become more active than usual, and prey upon adipose substances (500), forming a lymph which may have many of the characteristics of chyle, and serve the purposes of nutrition. But in ordinary operations, when the alimentary organs are supplied, the lymph is mainly an excrementitious substance.

506. Impurities accumulating by the return of worn-out matter to the circulation, and by absorption of substances unfitted for the system, are expelled by the excretory organs. The lungs (479) are largely concerned in this work. The liver (460) is associated in the same function; and the kidneys excrete a large proportion of effete impurities. The mucous membrane also participates in this office; but the external skin (331), exceeds all the other depurating organs in the *quantity* of matter which it *eliminates*. It is in some measure a respiratory organ, corresponding in function with the lungs (479). Like these, it consumes oxygen, and eliminates carbonic acid gas; also sensible perspiration. Unassimilated substances absorbed from the alimentary cavity are largely eliminated by the skin; and decomposed matter is continually passing off through this great limiting membrane (330). The opinion was advanced by Sanctorius, that the skin throws off, in the form of

E

insensible perspiration, something more than one-half of all the matter which enters the vital domain.

507. The depurating organs (289) reciprocate in function to a considerable extent, and in disease vicarious function is often attempted. Copious perspiration diminishes the secretion of the kidneys, and a suppression of the cutaneous functions increases that of the kidneys. The skin and lungs reciprocate in the same manner. Excessive excretions of the alimentary canal frequently result from a suppression of the function of the skin, and are always attended with cutaneous depression. But the welfare of the parts requires that each organ should uniformly perform its own duty; because excesses, arising from an undue determination of fluids to any one part, lead to debility, resulting in impaired function, imperfect assimilation, local disease, and general injury. Sudden suppressions of the functions of the skin lead to diabetes and pulmonary consumption, by causing undue determinations to the kidneys and lungs. The liver suffers from want of integrity in the other depurating organs; and its derangements compel the skin to throw off the matter which it should have eliminated.

508. In the healthful performance of their functions, the organs necessarily suffer waste of substance as well as expenditure of power (376). But while the economy of nutrition is sustained, the replenishment keeps pace with the exhaustion. By irregularities, and every means by which the constitutional laws are violated, not only is the system made to suffer, but the organs are made the seats of local disease.

509. Most of the human family know that the teeth become the seats of distressing decay; the gums may become flaccid and ulcerous. The tongue and the mouth are subject to disease in a variety of forms. The salivary fluid and mucous secretions may be rendered acrid and irritating; the salivary glands may become inflamed, enlarged, indurated, and cancerous; the nose, fauces, windpipe, meatpipe, etc., are liable to disease. The lungs are subject to inflammation, ulceration, and decay; the heart and blood-vessels are liable to enlargements, ruptures, ossification, etc. Derangement of function, formation of calculi, chronic inflammation, change of structure, a decay of substance, may take place in the liver, kidneys, etc. There is not an organ, tissue, or substance, which may not become diseased, and prove the source of death. The bones (185), may become brittle, or ulcerate, or mortify. The cartilages (185), ligaments (188), and tendons (195), may become dry, and lose their elasticity; the nerves and muscles may suffer change of structure, and decay of substance.

510. There are external causes by which diseases are induced; but the alimentary cavity is the principal avenue through which the causes commit their depredations; the stomach being a centre of irritation to the whole body. It is liable to be disturbed, and communicates its irritations to other organs (297, 298). Substances not adapted to the wants of the vital economy; alimentary substances, themselves proper, introduced in improper quantity, at an improper time, or without suitable mastication (426) become the causes of irritation. The passions, mental excitements, and severe mental application (304) also affect the stomach. In short, whatever impairs the nervous

power and muscular contractility of the stomach (444) tends to induce morbid irritability, inflammation, thickening of its coats, change of structure, scirrhus, cancer, etc. ; and disease may progress for years, terminating in death, without being suspected.

511. But the stomach does not suffer alone. All irritations impair the quality of the chyme, and all the fluids and solids of the body. The heart, lungs, liver, etc., sympathise (297, 298), and are disturbed. If, in consequence of hereditary peculiarities, any organ is predisposed to disease, these irritations tend to develope it ; when the local disease either reacts upon the stomach, and becomes a source of irritation to that organ, or serves as a kind of outlet, by which the irritations are relieved, and the stomach sustained at the expense of the diseased part which suffers from every error of diet. Thus, gastric irritation produces spinal irritation, which reacts on the stomach, and disease may be induced in the lungs, liver, etc., by gastric irritation, to the extinction of life, while the stomach seems in excellent health, and the sufferer is confident that nothing which he swallows does him any injury, because " it sits well on his stomach." In this manner, every organ may fall a sacrifice to the abuses of the alimentary canal ; and, fevers of every type, acute and chronic disease of every form, may spring from the same source.

IX.

(This lecture is chiefly occupied with an examination of Phrenology).

520. Whatever be the substratum of the sensorial brain, it acts through the nervous substance as if it were merely a property of that vitalised matter ; and all its powers are subject to the same laws as govern the manifestations of vitality. This truth is of immense importance. It lies at the foundation of intellectual and moral philosophy, and is of vital interest to human happiness.

522. In regard to the seat of the soul, different opinions have prevailed. The question is, whether the mind acts through the brain, as a single organ, or a system of organs. This has been made a prominent inquiry by the theory advanced by Gall, Spurzheim, and others (274, 279).

567. In perfect sleep, there is a suspension of the powers of the nerves (228, 229). When we dream, sleep is imperfect, from some nervous irritation, or some oppression in the body ; and the character of dreams corresponds with the nature of the irritation and the general condition of the nerves of organic life (228). Most frequently the exciting cause is irritation in the digestive organs (297, 298, 299).

571. When the system is healthy, sleep is death-like, and the organs of perception are, as it were, paralysed. The irritation which produces dreams may be carried to such an extent as will cause permanence of distinct conceptions, when awake, so that the mind will be engrossed with these, and abstracted from actual perceptions. The things conceived will be realities to the mind (568), and we shall think, feel, talk, and act, as if our conceptions were real perceptions ; and we shall be called insane.

572. The constant contemplation of things conceived, as realities, will establish new associations of thought, and thus lay the foundation for permanent

insanity. For intellectual habitudes are easily formed, and, when established, are with great difficulty broken up, especially those associated with feelings and propensities.

573. When nervous irritation is less violent, and developed in connection with qualifying circumstances, as loss of property, character, friends, &c., the morbid conceptions may be limited, and the case will be called *monomania*, or insanity on one subject.

579. Strict mental and moral sanity requires that our propensities, affections, emotions, or passions, should be equal to the importance of the subject contemplated, when compared with all other things of which we have any notion; or correspond with what is true in the nature of things. All departure from this is a deviation from strict sanity. He that desires, loves, hates, abhors, or estimates anything above or below its real worth, is in some degree insane.

580. This is one of the most important laws of the mind; and the disregard of it in education is the source of immense evil. It requires that every precaution be taken to prevent the association of an improper degree of affection with any perceptions, conceptions, or reflections; that when we think of supplying the wants of the body, of labour, pleasure, poverty, riches, dress, fame, life, death, virtue, vice, &c., our affection should correspond with the importance of the thing contemplated, and enable us to estimate each at its true value.

591. Though I do not wish to be considered as an opponent of the theory of Dr. Gall, I must contend that while the brain is the seat of thought, the phrenic nerves are so connected as its intellectual and moral instruments (590), and the operations of the brain are so closely associated (565) with the nerves of organic life (305), that the intellectual and moral philosophy of man cannot be understood without a knowledge of the nervous system as a whole; and it is only by attention to the physiological laws of the domain of organic life, that we can hope to have such an effect on the brain, and other parts, as will secure health, wisdom, virtue, and happiness.

X.

598. The lower animals have the sense of thirst, but neither the reasoning nor the power to supply this want with anything else but water, and, therefore, are satisfied with good water; but out of this man generates artificial wants, which exert their influence upon his intellectual and voluntary powers as his instinctive wants do, but with a more despotic energy, and a continual tendency to excess. The same is true of hunger: in the lower animals it is simple and natural; but man multiplies this want into a thousand artificial ones, which exert a controlling influence upon him. In the same manner, every other natural want is multiplied to the extent of man's capabilities (21); and out of these wants, ingrafted upon the propensities, spring a multitude of others in connection with the customs of society. These artificial wants are so intimately associated with the natural, that few know the difference between them; whilst all press their demands, urging those exercises of the voluntary powers by which they can be indulged.

599. But in thus multiplying his wants, man not only depraves the natural instincts, but also impairs his mental faculties, deteriorates his whole nature, and tends to the destruction of mind and body.

600. Hence, were man only elevated above the other animals by superior intellectual powers, his elevation would answer no other end than to increase the depth of his misery.

601. To prevent this tendency of man's animal nature, and to excite his intellectual powers to the attainments of knowledge and wisdom, he is endowed with MORAL POWERS, and made the subject of moral government.

603. The constitutional laws which govern the body, and on which its physiological powers depend, harmonise with those which govern his intellectual and moral nature. Hence no law can be adapted to the highest condition of man's moral nature which is not consistent with the physiological laws of his body ; and no bodily habit can be adapted to the best condition of his body which is not consistent with the laws of his intellectual and moral nature.

611. Every human being has something within him which approves or disapproves of specific moral actions and qualities. This is what men call *Conscience.* But this is neither a simple nor an innate faculty ; it is of a complex character, and wholly the result of education , and is with no certainty a rule of right.

612. The MORAL SENSE is an innate power, but is not to be confounded with the *conscience.* Its definite language is, " BE RIGHT!—BE RIGHT! " But what that right is, it has no power to ascertain. For this it depends on the intellectual faculties. Whatever the understanding, acting under the moral sense, determines to be true or right, the moral sense receives as right, and prompts the soul to obey.

615. But the moral sense may be cultivated as to its influence. It may be feeble from want of exercise, so that it will never urge the understanding to ascertain truth. It may also be impaired by violations of constitutional laws (603). Whatever impairs the sensorial power of the nervous system, commensurately impairs the moral sense ; and all intentional violation of the constitutional laws of man's moral nature impairs the moral sense. On the other hand, the moral sense may, by cultivation, be rendered vigorous, so that it will urge the understanding to act aright.

616. When the moral sense is inactive, it does not influence the understanding, but leaves it either to neglect, or unfairly weigh evidences, and thus form a false conscience. When, on the other hand, the moral sense is morbidly active, it throws so distracting an influence on the understanding as to impair its operations, and weaken its conclusions ; and thus the mind is kept in a state of perplexity, which only increases the insane energy of the moral sense.

620. It is a general law, that the ability to ascertain moral truth corresponds with the physiological and moral purity of the individual. Suppose we attempt to convince a man strongly addicted to the use of tobacco that it is wrong to use it. Tobacco has impaired his moral sense (615); impaired the understanding to perceive moral truth (599); and established an appetite whose despotic influence urges the WILL to comply with its demands (598). When,

therefore, we attempt to convince him that it is wrong, we shall find it difficult to reach his moral sense through the opposing energy of his lust, which
will not suffer his mind to fix its attention seriously on the evidence, but keep
it employed in contemplating the importance of the gratification. Or if we
succeed in forcing evidence upon him, his lust will not suffer his understanding to weigh that evidence with honesty. In this manner, every appetite
(598), according to its influence, tends to produce erroneous conclusions or
fallacious conscience.

624. True religion consists in perfectly obeying all the constitutional laws
of human nature; for this would be fulfilling our relation to God, our duty to
ourselves and to our fellow-creatures. Thus we should love God with all the
heart, soul, mind, and strength, and our fellow-creatures as ourselves. But
human nature has always come short of this fulfilment, and from the delin-
quency has sprung the evils that man experiences.

628. Finally. When the conclusions of the understanding are true, the
conscience is true; but if the understanding is brought to erroneous conclusions, the conscience is false. Consequently, the fact that a man is sincere is
no proof that he is right; nor is the fact that conscience does not reprove him
proof that he is not morally wrong.

629. Gall and Spurzheim make the brain of more exclusive importance than
I do (588), and attribute less to the physiological conditions of the nerves of
organic life. They study man more exclusively within the brain (592), while
I insist on the physiological laws of his whole organisation. They may be
correct in asserting that man has other innate moral faculties, such as benevo-
lence, veneration, &c. If there be such innate powers, it is certain that the
philosophy of them is precisely the same as that of the moral sense. And
with the application of this physiological philosophy to all the cerebral organs
described by Gall and Spurzheim, I should have less objection to their theory,
because it would thereby be rendered more consistent with truth.

XI.

631. Josephus assigns as a reason for the great longevity of the primitive
generations, that the human constitution was then vigorous and fresh from
the hands of the Creator, and the food of man was then fitter for the prolon-
gation of life.

632. There has been much speculation concerning the length of the years
spoken of by early historians, in reference to the period of human life in the
primitive ages. Hufeland thinks "it has been made to appear in the highest
degree probable that the year, till the time of Abraham, consisted only of
three months; that it was afterwards extended to eight; and that it was not
till the time of Joseph that it was made to consist of twelve." These asser-
tions are, in a certain degree, confirmed by some of the eastern nations, who
still reckon only three months to the year. The whole account, according to
this explanation, assumes a different appearance. The nine hundred years
which Methuselah lived will be reduced to two hundred; an age which is not
impossible.

636. It cannot be doubted that the primitive generations exceeded in length of life the present inhabitants of the earth. Nevertheless, for the last three thousand years, the limit of human life has remained pretty nearly the same.

638. The history of the race proves man to be so constituted, that those excesses which deprave his nature (599), and lead to the extermination of the species, so affect him in his social relations, as at the same time to impair his intellectual and moral powers, rendering him incapable of sustaining those institutions and political conditions by which he is protected, and fitting him to become an easy prey to the hardier portions of his race. The age of wealth brings luxury, sensuality, and excess. Disease admonishes in vain Pestilence peals a louder note of rebuke, till it seemed as if the race would be exterminated ; and only by such retributions have mankind been induced to investigate the obvious relations between their habits and their sufferings.

639. Indeed it seems as if the grand experiment of mankind had been to ascertain how far they can transgress the laws of life, and yet not die so suddenly as to be compelled to know they have destroyed themselves.

642. Each nation has had its period of longevity, its age of heroism, conquest, patriotism, legislative wisdom, political energy, wealth, luxury, &c. It is also true that the general average of life often runs low in a nation which at the same time has many instances of individual longevity.

644. Civilised life is best adapted to the development of the physical, intellectual, and moral capabilities of man, and not only health and happiness, but also the political prosperity and durability of nations are proportionate to the conformity of the people to the laws of life.

647. We have been told that some enjoy health in warm, and others in cold climates (15) ; some on one kind of diet, and under one set of circumstances, and some under another ; therefore, what is best for one is not for another ; what agrees *well* with one, disagrees with another ; what is one man's meat is another man's poison ; different constitutions require different treatment ; and, consequently, no rules can be laid down adapted to all circumstances which can be made laws of regimen to all.

651. Without taking pains to examine circumstances, people consider the bare fact that some intemperate individuals reach old age, evidence that such habits are not unfavourable to life. With the same loose reasoning, people arrive at conclusions equally erroneous, in regard to nations. If a tribe subsisting on vegetable food is weak, sluggish, and destitute of courage and enterprise, it is concluded that vegetable food is the cause. Yet examination might have shown that causes fully adequate to these effects existed, which not only exonerated the diet, but made it appear that the vegetable diet had a redeeming effect, and was the means by which the nation was saved from a worse condition.

654. The fact that individuals have attained a great age in certain habits of living is no evidence that those habits are favourable to longevity. The only use which we can make of cases of extraordinary old age, is to show how long the human constitution is capable of sustaining the vital economy, and resisting the causes which induce death.

657. If we ask *how* we must live to secure the best health and longest life, the answer must be drawn from physiological knowledge; but if we ask how long the the best mode of living will preserve life, the reply is, physiology cannot teach you that. Probably, each aged individual has a mixture of good and bad habits, and lived in a mixture of favourable and unfavourable circumstances. Notwithstanding apparent diversity, there is a pretty equal amount of what is salutary in the habits and circumstances of each. Some have been correct in one thing and some in another. Besides some, with powerful constitutions, may, in the constant violation of the laws of life, reach old age with as much vigour as others who attain the same in better circumstances, but with less powerful constitutions. All that is proved by instances of longevity in connexion with bad habits is, that such individuals are able to resist causes that have in the same time sent thousands of their fellow-creatures to an untimely grave; and, under a correct regimen, they would have sustained life perhaps a hundred and fifty years.

658. Some have more constitutional power to resist the causes of disease than others, and, therefore, what will destroy the life of one may be borne by another a long time without any manifestations of immediate injury. There are also constitutional peculiarities, but these are far more rare than is generally supposed. Indeed, such may in almost every case be overcome by a correct regimen. So far as the general laws of life and the application of general principles of regimen are considered, the human constitution is ONE; there are no constitutional differences which will not yield to a correct regimen, and thus improve the individual. Consequently, what is best for one is best for all.

660. " Herodicus was master of an academy," says Plato, " where youth were taught their exercise, and being himself delicate and infirm, he contrived to blend exercise with such dietetic rules as preserved his own feeble constitution from sinking under his complaints, and enabled him to protract his valetudinary existence to old age; and he did the same to many others of feeble and infirm constitutions." Louis Cornaro, a Venetian, had broken down his constitution at thirty-five, and become so infirm that he despaired of recovering health, or reaching the meridian of life; yet by reforming his habits he recovered health, and lived to be over a hundred. Moses Brown, of Providence, R.I., nearly 100 years old, enjoying uncommon health and activity for his age, informed me that from his birth he was feeble, and his constitution always delicate. He had three brothers, who were all remarkable for robust, powerful constitutions, yet neither of these reached seventy. At eighty-three, Moses Brown observed, " I was always a feeble, frail thing among my brothers, and had no expectation of out-living them; I am persuaded that if I had had the constitution of either, and lived as I have, I should be an active hale man at a hundred years old, and probably live to a hundred and twenty years in good health; but with my feeble constitution, I do not expect to exceed ninety years." He died of sickness from exposure, in his ninety-eighth year.

663. In the present condition of the race, there is a great inequality of constitutional power. Some individuals are born too feeble to sustain life a

single year; others have power enough to maintain the victory over the causes which induce death for a hundred and fifty years. Some are born without any tendency to disease, while others have the predisposition to particular disease of some kind.   But differences result from causes which man has the power to control; and it is certain that all can be removed by conformity to the laws of life for generations, and the human species brought to as great uniformity as to health and life as the lower animals.

664.   Physiological science affords no evidence that the human constitution is not capable of gradually returning to the primitive longevity of the species.

672.   If vivacity and cheerfulness be pleasing in childhood, why should they not continue to be so through life ?   The highest interests of our nature require that *youthfulness* should be prolonged.   And it is as capable of being preserved as life itself is, both depending on the same conditions.

673.   If there ever was a state of the human constitution which enabled it to sustain life for several hundred years, that state involved a harmony of relative conditions.   The vital processes were less rapid and more complete than at present; development was slower; organisation more perfect; childhood protracted; and the change from youth to manhood took place at a greater remove from birth.   Hence, if we now aim at long life, we can secure our object only by conformity to those laws by which youthfulness is prolonged.

676.   In early life, when the proportion of the fluids is greatest, and when the sensibities of the solids are most delicate, then also the natural activity and cheerfulness are greatest.

677.   If this physiological condition could be preserved, the same state would continue (305); and though, with changes in development, exuberance of vivacity subsides to the sobriety of manhood, yet cheerfulness ought to be preserved through life.

678.   If all the physiological laws are obeyed, the change in the proportion of solids and fluids (674) must take place, and the buoyancy of youth subside into the tranquility of age, but slowly, and the decline of life will be gradual.

680.   Violation of the laws of life not only hastens the change in the solids and fluids (674), but mischievously changes their *relative conditions*, developing unhealthy sensibilities: all the functions are impaired; childhood and vigorous manhood are abbreviated; depression, suffering, and untimely death invade every hour; and most of the few who reach premature old age at seventy or eighty, find it a period of decrepitude, in which the senses are impaired and the intellectual powers have sunk into decay.

XII.

688.   Blood can be elaborated from all vegetable and animal substances; every thing that liveth, as well as every vegetable, can be made meat for man; but the vital properties of the blood vary with the qualities of food, hence the blood holds a precise relation to the substances; and its vital constitution is more or less adapted to our organisation, according to the character of the substances on which we subsist.

686.   The *vital properties* of the tissues (312) (683) hold fixed relations to the blood; so that these properties always nicely vary with the character of

the blood ; and hence, whatever deteriorates the blood impairs the elasticity of the cellular tissue, the contractility of the muscular tissue, and powers of the nervous tissue.

687. The functions of the stomach hold precise relations to the substances and functions of all the other organs ; no organ can perform its function independently of the others ; and therefore, *no organ can be impaired without involving the whole system.*

689. Whatever impairs the sensorial powers of the nervous system (1126), and deteriorates any of the tissues of the body (686), impairs our sight, hearing, smell, taste, and touch.

690. In a perfectly undepraved state the organ of smell detects odours with accuracy, and discriminates between what is salutary or injurious. The faculty was given *not* only as a means of enjoyment, but to serve (596) in detecting the characters of external things in relation to life, by the odours which they impart.

691. The olfactory nerves are distributed over the lining membrane of the nose (399), through which the air passes into the lungs ; and detect odorous properties of the atmosphere unfriendly to life.

692. Odours which are delightful when properly diluted become oppressive when the air is too deeply freighted with them ; therefore, the crowding of flowers in gardens and houses is unfriendly to our physiological welfare. We cannot carry gratification beyond the constitutional purposes for which these senses were instituted, without finding suffering in our pursuit.

694. The organ of smell is also a sentinel to the alimentary canal (294), and enables us to discriminate between salutary and poisonous substances. But this sentinel may become so depraved as to lose the power of appreciating odours ; thus, snuff-takers deprave the sense and impair its power.

696. If a person with undepraved nerves comes into the vicinity of tobacco, he perceives the loathsome odour, detects its poisonous character, and finds himself urged to avoid it ; but if he thrusts some into his nose, his nerves give the alarm, and sneezing ensues as the means of expelling the offending cause. We may succeed in destroying the integrity of this important sentinel so completely, that it can no longer detect the poisonous character of the tobacco, but will delight in its stimulation with an intensity of morbid enjoyment equal to the depth of depravity to which the nerves are reduced. Yet, the character of the poison remains unaltered, and equally hostile to life.

697. The taste is an important sentinel to perceive the gustatory properties of substances, and to discriminate between what is salutary and what is pernicious. When the taste is undepraved, its discriminating power in man is equal to that of any other animal (19), so that he may be instinctively guided in the selection of food (425), (596, 597). But by debauching the gustatory nerve we soon destroy the power to discriminate, and the tissues become so conformed to the qualities of improper substances, that they delight in their stimulation more than in those which are healthful ; and thus, by destroying the integrity of this sentinel we are given up to believe a lie. Indeed, the organs may become so depraved, that they will receive the most pernicious substances as agreeable and salutary.

698. We have, in an undepraved taste, a delicate variety of gustatory enjoyment, equal to the natural variety of substances prepared for our nourishment.   So that when our diet is conformable to the constitutional laws of our nature, we promote health and also gustatory enjoyment of the purest kind.

699. Inseparable from constitutional capabilities for happiness are equal capabilities for evil ; for these powers of enjoyment, when depraved, become the ministers of disease and untimely death.   Hence the maxim, that what is agreeable and sits well upon the stomach is nourishing and conducive to health, is true, while the purity of our organs are preserved; but fatally fallacious when our organs are depraved.

701. Thus the tobacco-eater and spirit-drinker impair their gustatory powers ; and those who indulge in such poisons destroy their taste, and are only able to appreciate the degree of stimulation produced by those substances. High seasonings, indeed all artificial stimuli, produce similar effects.

702. Those, therefore, who seek for gustatory enjoyment in the preparations of culinary skill, defeat their object ; they diminish their enjoyment by such means, and circumscribe it to narrower limits, in proportion as they depart from that simplicity required by the constitutional laws.

706. The teeth are constituted with fixed relations to the nature of the substances designed for human aliment ; and if their laws of constitution and relation be obeyed, the teeth will never become diseased.   The teeth are among the last organs which manifest the deteriorations or meliorations of the constitution ; hence some may violate the laws of nature in a manner calculated to destroy their teeth, and yet die with sound teeth ; but, if the same habits be continued, the third or fourth generation will be afflicted with miserable teeth.   On the other hand, people with teeth predisposed to decay, may observe the constitutional laws without being able to preserve their teeth from disease ; yet they will preserve them longer than they would other-wise last, and suffer little pain ; and, if these habits are persevered in, the third or fourth generation will have excellent teeth.

707. Those alimentary substances which the best interests of the teeth require, are also conducive to the best interests of the whole vital domain.

709. Our teeth being formed to cut and grind our food (328), every substitute for their legitimate use is an infraction of their laws of constitution and relation, and results in commensurate injury.   But when their function is correctly performed, on the right substances in the right condition, the laws of constitution and relation are obeyed, and the healthful condition of the teeth preserved.   Almost all artificial preparations are injurious to the teeth.

711. A sea captain, who observed the teeth of different nations, found that where the people use much hot drink and hot food, and smoke tobacco or other narcotic substances, their teeth are black and much decayed ; but in the islands of the Pacific, where the people seldom take anything hot into their mouths, and are simple and natural in their diet, their teeth were regular and free from decay.

713. Culinary preparations lead us to masticate too little, to swallow too fast (416), and eat too much. By eating our food in a natural state, or with that preparation which still requires full mastication, we avoid all these evils, and preserve the teeth.

714. The enamel is a species of organic crystalization (327), destitute of nerves and sensibility ; yet its condition is connected with the health of the bony substance which it surrounds (423). The bony portion is supplied with vessels and nerves, capable of morbid sensibility ; and the fact that disease of the teeth is attended with pain, is a demonstration that such disease is organic, and originates in the bony portion by inflammation. Among the causes acting on the teeth, heat is the most powerful. It is common to hear people speak of substances as injurious ; but if these were never swallowed, the teeth would suffer little from them. If the food is soft and hot, concentrated, high-seasoned, or otherwise vicious, and mastication is neglected, tartar will gather around the teeth, irritate the gums, separate them from the enamel, and irritate the membrane which surrounds the roots (323). Decay will follow, and the teeth must be lost, unless the progress of the disease is arrested by correct habits.

715. The teeth do not suffer alone. The gums and salivary glands, as well as the mouth, taste, and alimentary canal, are involved in the injury, and react upon the teeth.

716. When the food is properly masticated and mixed with saliva, it under-goes a change, approaching the character of chyme ; hence the more com-pletely the functions of the mouth are performed, the more is the food fitted for the stomach. The quality of the saliva may be varied by the different conditions of the glands, which depend on the kind of stimulation which induces their secretion. Imperfect mastication also becomes a source of irritation to the stomach, which reacts upon the salivary glands.

718. Everything unfriendly to the constitution and health of the teeth is far more pernicious to them in childhood than in later periods of life (227). There is no period in which the teeth are so injured as previous to their appearance above the gums. During the development of the temporary teeth (323, 324), the germs of the permanent teeth are formed, and these germs participate in all the affections of the system through the nerves of organic life (225). During the progress of second dentition, every disturbing cause in the organic domain strikes at the very constitution of the teeth, preparing them for early decay.

719. Calomel, and all medicine which has a general effect on the system, is often destructive to the permanent teeth, before these are formed. Every-thing in the dietetic habits also which is stimulating, producing feverish-ness, and calculated to hasten second dentition, has an unhealthy effect on the teeth. Hence it is of importance that the diet of children should be simple, and every measure taken to preserve the general health.

720. The skin is of much importance as an organ of respiration (506) ; and there are similar laws of relation between the skin and the atmosphere, as between the lungs and atmosphere.

722. The body derives nourishment from the atmosphere (470), and wo cannot live many minutes without a supply. Oxygen is the nutritious principle of the air ; azote is innutritious. Pure air contains one part of nourishment with four of innutritious substance ; and the lungs receive this large proportion of innutritious, for the sake of the portion of nutritious substance which they appropriate by a vital process, which may be called pulmonary digestion (471).

723. Considering the rage for concentrated and stimulating substances, would it not be an excellent plan to establish laboratories for procuring as much oxygen as mankind require, and thus save the laborious task of separating the nutritious principle of the atmosphere from such a large quantity of innutritious matter ? But such an artificial preparation would be ruinous to the lungs. If we were to breathe pure oxygen, there would be greatly increased action : the lungs and other organs would become inflamed, and the vital powers soon destroyed. In proportion as the air deviates to an excess of oxygen, the vital exhaustion of our system is increased and life is abbreviated. And in proportion as the air deviates to an excess of azote, respiration becomes imperfect, the lungs lose their healthy tone, and the system tends to decay. When these deviations are small, and gradually increase, we may not be sensible that the air is not best adapted to our lungs. Nevertheless all such deviations are injurious.

726. The nerves of the stomach perceive the stimulus of every substance received, and convey the impression to the centre (220) which presides over the stomach, according to the character of the stimulus (429).

727. In a healthy state this sensibility enables it to detect both the *quality of the stimulus* and the *degree of stimulation*, and to discriminate between substances best adapted to the system and those which are pernicious, or less adapted. When the quality and quantity are best adapted to the vital interests, the stimulation is diffused over the system (297), and we have an animal consciousness of a buoyancy of spirits (305).

728. But this organic sense may be depraved or destroyed, so that the stomach may become destitute of the power to appreciate the *quality* of the stimulus, and be reduced to the mere ability to appreciate the *degree* of its stimulation. It may even be made to prefer those substances which are pernicious.

729. By direct sympathetic irritations, the whole system is made to partake of this depravity, so that pernicious substances may be habitually thrown into the gastric cavity, and rapidly or slowly destroy the constitution (448). We may remain unconscious of this state of things, and contend for the safety of our habits on the ground that our stomachs are satisfied. In *post-mortem* examination extensive disease has been found pervading the stomach and intestines, which indicated a progress of many years, yet the subject was not sensible of its existence.

732. The morbid irritability of a depraved stomach renders it capricious, and causes it to reject or receive things without any regard to the interests of the vital economy ; the healthy sensibilities of an undepraved stomach, on the

other hand, cause it to receive with satisfaction those substances which are adapted to the vital economy, and to reject, or complain of, those substances which are unfriendly.

733. In relation to the digestive organs, every substance from which the body can derive nourishment possesses a stimulating quality, proportionate to its quantity. Some are more nourishing and less stimulating than others ; others more stimulating and less nourishing; and some stimulating without affording any nourishment.

734. By the stimulating properties of food our digestive organs are excited to the performance of their functions ; and suffer a commensurate exhaustion (376). But replenishment is continually carried on to counteract these effects and sustain the organs (393). If the excitement is intense the exhaustion is too rapid and the organ debilitated (508).

735. Substances, the stimulating power of which is barely sufficient to excite a healthy action of the digestive organs, are most conducive to the welfare of the body, causing no unnecessary expenditure of vital power. For every degree of stimulating power beyond this the organs would be more exhausted, assimilation more rapidly performed (634), and life shortened.

736. It is, therefore, one of the most important physiological laws that that aliment which is assimilated with the least expense of vital power is most conducive to health and long life (634).

737. All substances designed for human aliment are composed of both nutritious and innutritious matter, and the stomach and intestines are constituted to receive substances so composed (428). Too great a proportion of nutritious matter is little less dangerous to our digestive organs than too small. If the stomach had been designed to receive nutritious matter only the intestinal tube would be unnecessary. But it is the duty of the alimentary canal to receive proper substances, after they have been thoroughly masticated, to separate and convert the nutritious matter into chyme (428), and to remove the innutritious residuum (446).

738. If we supply the alimentary organs with concentrated nutritious matter only, we shall soon destroy the functional powers, causing atrophy and death.

739. Some animals require a greater proportion of innutritious matter than others, but all require some, and all correct experiments confirm its truth. Thus, dogs fed on sugar and water will die ; but if a considerable proportion of sawdust be mixed with the sugar they will not die, but thrive. Dogs fed on fine flour bread and water will die in about seven weeks ; but if on unbolted wheat-meal bread and water, they will live. An ass fed on rice will die in about fifteen days, but if a quantity of straw be mixed with the rice he will thrive. Horses fed exclusively on grain will die in a short time, but mix a suitable proportion of straw or wood shavings, and they will become fat. Horses fed on grain alone instinctively gnaw the boards within reach.

[*Several facts are quoted of horses having been saved at sea, by mixing shavings with their corn after the hay had been lost in rough weather.*]

744. Children whose food consists of fine flour bread and other concentrated substances, such as sugar, butter, &c., become weak and often afflicted with

disease. But a child, upon good bread made of wheat meal, with milk or pure soft water for drink, and fruits, will be healthy and robust.

745. It is a common remark among whalemen that, during their long voyages, the coarser their bread the better their health.

[*Examples of injury from the use of concentrated food, and the case of Dr. Stark, who died, 1774, after several absurd experiments, are here given.*]

747. Many have subsisted for years on coarse bread and water alone, and become remarkably vigorous ; but no human being ever injured his health by simple diet, adapted in kind and condition to the alimentary organs.

748. Debility, constipation, and morbid irritability of the alimentary canal, set up by concentrated food, compound preparations, irritating stimuli, and excess, have been always the principal causes of disease.

754. A pound of wheat contains about ten ounces of farina, six drachms of gluten, and two drachms of sugar ; and a man may be sustained on one pound of wheat per day, with pure water ; but let him attempt to live on ten ounces of pure farina, six drachms of gluten, and two drachms of sugar per day, and he will soon find his strength failing, and death will terminate his experiment in less than a year. Chemistry cannot tell us why ; but Physiology tells us that wheat is adapted to the alimentary organs, though concentrated farina, gluten, and sugar are not ; therefore, the wheat, while it affords nourishment, also sustains the organs in digesting that nourishment ; but pure farina, gluten, and sugar break down the alimentary organs and cause the system to perish.

756. Therefore, there are fixed laws of relation between the alimentary organs and those substances designed for food, so that it is certain that there are kinds best adapted to sustain the highest condition of human nature.

757. The special sense of hunger in a healthy system gives warning when the vital economy requires a supply, and asks for food, but has no power to discern what is best,—for this it depends on other senses (691, 697, 698). In a depraved state of the stomach (728) the integrity of this sense is destroyed, and the feeling which we call hunger is no evidence that the vital economy requires food. It is a morbid craving for stimulation (697), which returns, with more or less capriciousness, according to the habits and condition of the system. This kind of hunger is as likely to be felt when no food is required as when needed ; nor will food satisfy such a stomach unless it contains the customary stimulus.

XIII.

758. From the laws of constitution and relation we perceive that the more natural the food of man, the more healthy will be the body, the more perfect the senses, and the more active may the intellectual and moral faculties be rendered (765).

760. Man possesses a capability of educating himself to artificial modes of life ; but, in so doing, he impairs the physiological powers of his constitution.

764. It is obvious that *the natural state of man* is that in which his organic and animal powers are kept in conformity to the physiological laws, and in which his intellectual and moral powers are best cultivated.

766. In turning to history, many perplexing difficulties meet us, and nothing but science and investigation can save us from being misled.

767. The present condition of the human family is a fair specimen of what it has been for several thousand years. Portions of the race are found in the torrid, temperate, and frigid zones (15). Some subsist on vegetable food, others on a mixture of vegetable and animal, and others entirely on animal.

768. Tobacco is freely used, alcohol is scarcely less universal, and opium is consumed in nearly an equal quantity. Tea, coffee, and other deleterious stimulants are considered almost as necessary as air. Besides, the bad passions, irregularities, want of moral cultivation, and other things, militate continually against the physiological welfare of those whose dietetic habits may be simple, and prevent the advantages which would otherwise flow from such a diet. No facts of this kind, therefore, ought to be considered as of any weight against physiological principles.

769. All the writers of antiquity assert that the first generations of men (631) were natural and simple in their diet.

[Quotations in proof are given from the writings of Moses, Sanchoniathon, Hesiod, Pythagoras, Herodotus, Hippocrates, Diodorus Siculus, Ovid, Ælianus, Pliny, Plutarch, Galen, Porphyry, &c.]

771. Fruits. nuts, farinaceous seeds, and roots, with perhaps some milk, and it may be honey, in all probability, constituted the food of the first generations of mankind.

772. These articles were, at first, received in their natural state, witho t any preparation. But as change of seasons taught the necessity of providenc , and seeds became hard by keeping, they naturally had recourse to mashing on flat stones. By use these stones became hollowed. This led to the manufacture of mortars for preparing dry articles of food, probably sometimes parched, and afterwards, perhaps, wet up into a coarse dough and baked.

774. With habits such as these, unblighted by hereditary taint, and little enervated by ancestral sensuality, it is no marvel that the antediluvians should average several centuries of life (634).

775. With all the deteriorations of six thousand years (638, 643), the human constitution even yet, where circumstances, conditions, and habits concur to fulfil the physiological laws, has power to climb towards primitive longevity, with much of primitive vigour (673).

776. Captain Cook found evidence of the healthiness of the New Zealanders in the great number of very old men, none of them decrepit (678). "They did not come in the least behind the young in cheerfulness and vivacity."

[Paragraphs 777 and 778 show that the North American Indians and the Pampa Indians in the South were found much in the same state.]

779. Some of the Arabs subsist on the milk of their camels. These have no sickness, and attain great age with vigour and activity (678). Captain Riley thinks he met with some who were three hundred years old; and many who were strong and active at two hundred.

782.—Before the discovery of the Ladrone Islands about 1620, the inhabitants supposed themselves the only people in the world, and were destitute of almost everything that people in civic life think necessary. They had never seen fire. Their food was fruits and roots in a natural state. They were well formed, vigorous, and active, and could carry with ease upon their shoulders a weight of five hundred pounds. Disease was scarcely known, and they generally attained to a great age.

[*Other examples of longevity are given in the Maltese, Russians, Brahmins of India, Essenes among the Jews, members of the Society of Friends, &c.*]

797. In all these cases there is still so wide a departure from physiological rectitude (764), that the results are greatly modified. They show, however, that the more diet is adapted in simplicity (765) to the constitutional laws, the more perfectly the interests of nature are sustained (758).

XIV.

803. Man possesses the capability of deriving nourishment from almost everything in the vegetable and animal kingdoms ; but do the highest interests of the human constitution require that man should subsist on both vegetable and animal food ?

817. In the human head (326) there are thirty-two teeth : eight incisors, four cuspids or eye teeth, eight bicuspids or small cheek teeth, and twelve molars or large cheek teeth ; and the teeth of each jaw form an uninterrupted series, in close juxtaposition, and all of nearly equal length. In this man differs from other animals. In the species nearest to man there is a space between the front and the corner teeth ; while in other species, both carnivorous and herbivorous, the space is greater between the incisors and the cuspids, and between these latter and the cheek teeth. Carnivorous animals have in each jaw six incisors or front teeth, two cuspids, and from eight to twelve cheek teeth. Gnawing animals, as the rat, the beaver, the squirrel, &c., have two incisors in each jaw, no cuspids, and from six to ten cheek teeth. Ruminating animals without horns, as the camel, dromedary, &c., have two upper and six lower incisors, from two to four cuspids, and from ten to twelve cheek teeth in each jaw. Ruminating animals with horns, as the ox, sheep, &c., have no upper incisors, eight lower incisors, no cuspids, except in the stag, which has them in the upper jaw, and twelve cheek teeth in each jaw. Animals with undivided hoofs, as the horse, have six incisors in each jaw, two cuspids in the upper jaw, none in the lower, and twelve cheek teeth in each.

818. The body of the human tooth above the gum (327) consists of bone, everywhere covered with enamel. In this man resembles both carnivorous and frugivorous animals, and differs from the herbivorous, whose teeth are composed of intermixed layers of bone and enamel.

819. The incisors of the human head are broad, chisel-shaped teeth, to cut the substances for the action of the cheek teeth. The front teeth of carnivorous animals are pointed, and stand farther apart, bearing no resemblance to those of man. The incisors of herbivorous animals are broad, but they are stronger, the cutting ends more blunt ; and in some species they vary almost as widely from those of man as the carnivorous.

F

820. The corner or eye teeth in the human head are the same length as the front teeth (326), and close to them. They approach to a point; but their shape indicates nothing more than that they constitute the first steps of transition from the cutting teeth to the square grinders. The cuspids or tusks of carnivorous animals are pointed, much longer and stronger than the front teeth, and separated by a considerable space both from the front and cheek teeth. In some species these are long and powerful, obviously fitted to serve as weapons, and used to seize, hold, and tear the prey. Some of the herbivorous animals, as the horse, camel, and stag (817) have the cuspids longer, more pointed, and powerful than the corner teeth of the human head, and they are separated from the other teeth. In the camel the cuspids bear a strong resemblance to those of predaceous animals.

821. Between the cuspids of carnivorous animals and the corner teeth of the human head there is not the slightest resemblance ! If the assumed resemblance had some reality the argument would equally prove that the horse, camel, &c., require flesh-meat (820). But the assumed resemblance has no reality, therefore the reasoning founded upon it is fallacious.

822. The bicuspids, or small cheek teeth, have two prominences (326). The molars, or large cheek or double teeth, have large square crowns, presenting grinding surfaces, with four or five blunt prominences (326). The bicuspids of carnivorous animals have two or three sharp points, resembling saw-teeth ; and these points are not situated like the blunt tubercles of the human bicuspids, but one before the other, like the teeth of a saw, fitted for cutting and tearing. The large double teeth of carnivorous animals also rise into sharp points, the middle point of each rising like a spear. These present nothing which approaches to a grinding surface, but are fitted for cutting, and cannot admit of lateral motion. The molar teeth of herbivorous animals have very large, oblong-square crowns ; not proportionally larger than those of man, but their construction is different (818). A roughness is given to the grinding surface, which increases its dividing power upon the grass, twigs, and other substances on which herbivorous animals subsist.

823. The cheek teeth in the lower jaw of man shut against those of the upper jaw, so as to bring the grinding surfaces together, and thus grind the substances. In this, man resembles herbivorous and frugivorous animals. But the cheek teeth in the lower jaw of carnivorous animals shut within the upper ; so that a pair of shears, with the two cutting edges like saws, give a good idea of the cheek teeth of carnivorous animals. The manner in which these shut fits them for cutting flesh preparatory for swallowing, and precludes all lateral motion in mastication.

824. In herbivorous animals the joint of the lower jaw admits of lateral motion, as we see in the cow when chewing the cud. In man also, the under jaw admits of lateral motion (323), so that the surfaces of the upper and lower jaws can move upon each other, and grind the food (426). But in carnivorous animals lateral motion is precluded by the shutting of the lower cheek teeth within the upper (823), and by the articulation of the jaw, which only admits

of the backwards and forwards motion. In this respect man resembles herbivorous animals, and differs from the carnivorous.

825. The masticatory organs of carnivorous animals are fitted to seize and hold the prey, to tear the flesh, and cut it small enough to be swallowed ; and being raw, it passes less rapidly through the stomach, and sustains the animal a longer time than if it were finely ground. But the masticatory organs of man are fitted to grind the food and mix them with the saliva, which best fits it for the human stomach (717).

828. The salivary glands (340) of herbivorous animals are comparatively larger than those of the carnivorous. In man these are not so large as in herbivorous, nor so small as in carnivorous animals ; but they are copious in their secretion, and approach nearer to those of the former than the latter.

829. The average length of the alimentary canal is relatively much less in carnivorous than in herbivorous animals. In those animals which subsist on animal food its length varies from one to six or eight times the length of the body, with some exceptions. In herbivorous animals with undivided hoofs, as the horse, the canal varies from eight to eleven times the length of the body. In those that divide the hoof and chew the cud, as the ox, deer, sheep, &c., it varies from eleven to twenty-eight times the length of the body.

830. In ascertaining this length, naturalists have taken the body from the snout to the extremity of the back bone, but in man they have measured from the head to the heel ; and made it to appear that the length in man varies from three to eight times the length of the body. But if compared, in the same manner as in all other animals, it is ten or twelve times the length.

831. Carnivorous animals have a simple stomach, not fitted to retain the food long ; while the herbivorous have a complicated stomach (319), or a simple one, formed to retain its food longer. The human stomach is simple, but not more so than that of the horse, and it is formed to retain the food a considerable time (347). The large intestine in carnivorous animals is never cellulated, and comparatively small. In herbivorous animals, especially where the stomach is simple, this intestine is capacious, and the cœcum (346) particularly large ; whilst the colon is gathered into cells. In man the cœcum is large, and the colon (346) cellulated. Indeed, the diameter of the whole alimentary canal is relatively greater in man than in carnivorous animals ; moreover, the semilunar folds (346) in the small intestines considerably increase the longitudinal extent of the human canal.

833. No one claims man to be a *carnivorous*, but an *omnivorous* animal, as both the hog and the bear are naturally omnivorous ; that is, they will eat both vegetable and animal food. When free to choose, however, these prefer vegetable to animal substances, and neither of them ever preys upon living animals, unless urged by hunger.

834. There is no resemblance between the front teeth of the hog and those of the human head ; still less between the eye teeth and the tusks. The bicuspids of the hog are almost exactly like those of carnivorous animals. The molars, on the other hand, are like those of the human head. This comparison, therefore, does not show man to be omnivorous. The only teeth in the hog

which have any resemblance to human teeth indicate a frugivorous character.

825. The digestive organs of the hog more resemble those of man, but when taken in connection with the masticatory organs, and also with the fact that the hog prefers vegetable food, the evidence goes to prove that man is not naturally a flesh-eating animal.

836. In the order next below man, we find animals with organs nearly resembling those of the human body ; so that few, not acquainted with comparative anatomy, would detect the differences. The number and order of the teeth in the orang outang are the same as in man. The incisors are precisely like those of the human head ; the cuspids are relatively longer, separated from the other teeth (817), and approach more to the cuspids of carnivorous animals. The cheek teeth so much resemble the human, that it is difficult to distinguish them. The articulation of the jaw, form of the stomach, length of the alimentary canal, capacity of the coecum, and cellular arrangement of the colon in the orang outang, all correspond with those of the human body ; the comparative length of the canal, however, is somewhat greater in man.

837. In other species of monkeys the cuspids are longer, and the cheek teeth more pointed than in the orang outang. In the baboon the cuspids are long and powerful, resembling the corresponding teeth in carnivorous animals.

838. The alimentary organs of the orang outang, then, are the type (813) with which to compare those of the human body, to ascertain the natural dietetic character of man. But (836), in all that the organs differ, they bring the orang between man and carnivorous animals, and thus push man farther from a carnivorous character (813). Yet the orang outang, and other monkeys, are *frugivorous*, subsisting on fruits, nuts, and esculent farinaceous vegetables. They never feed on animal food, except in circumstances in which even the cow and the sheep become carnivorous.

839. The orang outang, on being domesticated, readily learns to eat animal food. But, if this proves that animal to be omnivorous, then the horse, cow, sheep, &c. are all omnivorous ; for every one of them is easily trained to eat animal food. "In Norway, some parts of Hadramant and the Coromandel coasts, the cattle are fed upon the refuse of fish, which fattens them readily, but seems totally to change their nature, and renders them ferocious."—(*Life of Reginald Heber, Harper's Family Library, No.* 40, *p.* 360.) Horses have frequently been trained to eat animal food ; and sheep have been so accustomed to it as to refuse grass.

840. So the lion, tiger, and other carnivorous animals, may be trained to a vegetable diet ; and if the young of these animals be trained to a vegetable diet till they are grown up, they will discover no desire for flesh.

841. All carnivorous animals can be trained to a vegetable diet, and brought to subsist thereon with less inconvenience and deterioration than herbivorous and frugivorous animals can be brought to live on animal food.

842. Comparative anatomy, therefore, proves that man is naturally a *frugivorous* animal, formed to subsist upon fruits, seeds, and farinaceous vegetables.

vegetables.—[*Quotations agreeing in this conclusion are given from Linnæus, Sir Everard Home, Cuvier, Lawrence, Bell, &c.*]

854. Although every animal organ has its precise constitutional character (687), yet it is capable of varying from its natural adaptation, and still not so far to impair its functional power as to interrupt the vital economy. Whenever the system is disturbed, every organ endeavours to adapt itself to the circumstances.

855. Possessing these powers, the human stomach, supplied with vegetable diet, will secrete a fluid qualified for its digestion ; and if changed to one of flesh-meat exclusively, the stomach will not at first be able to digest it. Yet if commenced by degrees, the stomach will become adapted to it.

856. If this adaptability were peculiar to the human stomach, it would go far to prove that man is naturally an omnivorous animal ; but when we know that it is common to the horse, ox, sheep (839), lion, tiger, cat, dog (840), and all the higher classes of animals (841), we see that it proves nothing but the wonderful resources of animated nature. Both carnivorous and herbivorous, as well as frugivorous animals, possess this versatility of digestive power: The sheep may even become so accustomed to a flesh diet as to refuse its natural food (839), (855).

857. Although the stomach possesses the power of adapting itself to various alimentary substances, according to the character of the diet, yet the stomach is nct capable of secreting a fluid which is equally well qualified to digest both vegetable and animal substances.

858. Children not much accustomed to flesh-meat eat every variety of fruits and vegetables with freedom ; but, as they become used to flesh-meat, their use of vegetable substances, except bread, rice, potatoes, or some other simple farinaceous article, becomes more circumscribed. Yet these, by an abandonment of flesh, may soon return to their enjoyment of fruits and vegetables.

863. Though herbivorous animals (839), can be trained to eat flesh and drink spirit till they learn to prefer them, such practices must be detrimental to those animals ; nor would they be less so if the rational powers of man were superadded to the instincts of the brute.

865. If man is not organised to eat flesh (846) no power of reason can render it suitable for him, or make him *naturally* an omnivorous animal ; nor can it make him artificially so without detriment to his nature. The question is not to what substances man can contrive so to adapt himself as to believe they are comfortable, but what substances are adapted to the vital interests of his system ?

866. The evidence of comparative anatomy proves that man is naturally frugivorous (842). The capability to subsist on a mixed diet is not peculiar to man, but common to all the higher animals (856). Reason is not a substitute for instinct, but superadded to act in supplying the wants of the body. Therefore the rationality of man neither lifts him above the laws of his nature, nor enables him to transgress those laws with impunity (763).

867. Man *can subsist* almost entirely on animal food (778), and a considerable

portion of the human family have partaken of it freely. Hence, it is inferred that he has the capability of subsisting with equal benefit upon both kinds of aliment ; that the diet is to be determined by climate, and that food will be best which is most congenial to the climate : vegetable in the torrid zone, animal in the frigid zones, or a mixture of the two in the temperate zones.

868. But (857) this capability being common to carnivorous, herbivorous, and frugivorous animals, cannot prove man to be naturally omnivorous.

869. Men *feel* their way to conclusions, and consult their appetites more than they examine evidence. Tobacco is quite as extensively used as flesh-meat (768), and those accustomed to the use of it would a thousand times sooner relinquish flesh than tobacco.

871. Certain faculties of instinct, preserved in their integrity, are a law of truth to all ; but they are capable of being depraved into blind guides, which lead to pernicious errors (694, 697).

875. The action of all extrinsic agents (126) tends to exhaust our vital properties ; and all intrinsic operations have an exhausting effect upon the organs (376). Even in the functions of nutrition each organ suffers some waste from its action (687). Hence all our operations carry on the two pro-cesses of exhaustion and repletion, destruction and renovation (314).

877. The more prodigally we expend the vital powers of our organs, the more rapidly we exhaust the limited stock of life (875). Nothing can be more fallacious than the opinion that our daily trespasses are as the dropping of water upon a rock—wearing indeed, but so imperceptibly as scarcely to make a difference in the duration of our lives.

878. Some alimentary substances are more stimulating than others, in pro-portion to the quantity of nourishment which they afford, and some are stimulating without affording any nourishment (735).

879. The stimulation produced is exhausting to the tissues in proportion to its degree ; and every stimulus impairs the vital powers in proportion as it is unfitted for the wants of the vital economy.

880. But whatever its character, every stimulation increases what is called the tone of the parts on which it is exerted, and, *while the stimulation lasts, increases the feeling of strength,* whether nourishment be imparted or not.

881. Yet by so much as the stimulation exceeds that which is necessary for the performance of the functions of the organs, the more does the expenditure of vital power exceed the renovating economy (502) ; and the exhaustion which succeeds is commensurate with the excess (735).

882. Hence, though food which contains the greatest proportion of stimu-lating power causes a *feeling* of the greatest strength, it also produces the greatest exhaustion, which is commensurately importunate for relief, and as the same food affords such by supplying the requisite stimulation, our feelings lead us to believe that it is the most strengthening.

883. Whenever a *less* is substituted for a *more* stimulating diet, a corres-ponding depression or want of tone succeeds, varying according to the condition of the system and suddenness of the change ; and this depression is attended

by a feeling of weakness, which is removed, and vigour restored, by the accustomed *degree* of stimulation, whether nourishment be afforded or not.

884. Stimulants (733), which afford no nourishment, and only increase waste of substance (735), cause a sense of strength. Thus we are led to believe that pure stimulants are strengthening.

886. Those substances the stimulating power of which is barely sufficient to excite the digestive organs in the appropriation of nourishment, are most conducive to the vital welfare (735), causing all the processes to be most perfectly performed, without any unnecessary expenditure (875), thus contributing to health and longevity.

890. Flesh-meat averages about thirty-five per cent of nutritious matter, while rice, wheat, and several kinds of pulse, such as lentils, peas, and beans, afford from eighty to ninety-five per cent. Potatoes afford twenty-five per cent of nutritious matter. So that a pound of rice contains more nutritious matter than two pounds and a half of meat; three pounds of wheat bread contain more than six pounds of flesh; and three pounds of potatoes more than two pounds of flesh.

[*Instances the Hebrews, Hindoos, Chinese, &c., as using little animal food.*]

897. "Children of the sun!" said one of the ancient and distinguished priests of India, "listen to the dying advice of your faithful and affectionate instructor, who hastens to the bosom of the great Allah, to give an account, and to enjoy the expected rewards of his services. Your regimen ought to be simple and inartificial. Drink only the pure, simple water. It is the beverage of nature, and not by any means nor in any way to be improved by art. Eat only fruits and vegetables! Let the predaceous animals prey on carnage and blood! Stain not the divine gentleness of your natures by one spark of cruelty to the creatures beneath you! Heaven, to protect them, hath placed you at their head! Be not treacherous to the important trust you hold, by murdering those you ought to preserve! nor defile your bodies by filling them with putrefaction! There is enough of vegetables and fruits to supply your appetites, without oppressing them by carrion, or drenching them in blood!"

899. The early inhabitants of Greece and Rome, and of Europe generally, subsisted almost entirely on vegetable food. The Spartan simplicity of diet was by no means peculiar to Sparta nor to Greece. "The Romans encouraged the use of vegetable diet, not only by the private example and precepts of many of their great men, but also by their public laws concerning food, which allowed but very little flesh, but permitted without limitation all kinds of food gathered from the earth, from shrubs, and from trees."

900. Plutarch writes: "I think it were better to accustom ourselves from our youth to such temperance as not to require any flesh-meat at all. Does not the earth yield abundance, not only for nourishment, but for luxury? some of which may be eaten as nature has produced it, and some dressed and made palatable in a thousand ways."

901. The inhabitants of modern Europe to a great extent subsist on the products of the vegetable kingdom. The peasantry of Norway, Sweden, Denmark, Poland, Germany, Turkey, Greece, Italy, Switzerland, Spain, France,

Portugal, England, Scotland, Ireland, a considerable portion of Russia, and other parts of Europe subsist mainly on vegetable food. The peasantry of modern Greece subsist on coarse brown bread and fruits. "In all the world," says a recent traveller in Italy, "there is not to be found a more lively mercurial population than the lazzaroni and labourers of Naples, whose diet is of the simplest kind, consisting mainly of bread, macaroni, or potatoes, or the fruits of the season, including a large supply of water-melons for their greatest luxury, with water for their drink. They are generally tall, stout, well-formed, robust, and active men." The peasantry in many parts of Russia live on very coarse bread, with garlics and other vegetables; and, like the same class in Greece, Italy, &c., they are obliged to be extremely frugal even in this kind of food; yet they are healthy, vigorous, and active. Many of the inhabitants of Germany live mainly on rye and barley, in the form of coarse bread. The Swiss peasantry subsist in much the same manner; and a very similar diet sustains the same class of people in Sweden, Poland, Spain, Portugal, and many parts of France.

902. The potato is the principal article in the diet of the Irish peasantry; and few portions of the human family are more healthy, athletic, and active when uncontaminated by intoxicating substances. But alcohol, tobacco, opium, coffee, and tea have extended their blighting influence (768) over the greater portion of the world; and nowhere do these scourges more cruelly afflict the self-devoted race than in the cottages of the poor. And when by these indulgences, and the neglect of cleanliness (872), &c., they generate diseases, sometimes extensive epidemics, we are told that these evils arise from their *poor, meagre, low, vegetable diet.* Whenever these different species of intoxicating substances are avoided, and a decent degree of cleanliness observed, the vegetable diet is not thus calumniated.

903. That portion of the peasantry of England and Scotland who subsist on their barley and oatmeal bread, porridge, potatoes, and other vegetables, with temperate, cleanly habits, is able to endure more fatigue and exposure than any other class of people in the same countries.

904. Three-fourths of the whole human family, in all periods of time, have subsisted on vegetable food; and when their supplies have been abundant, and their habits in other respects correct, they have been well nourished.

905. But if one pound of good bread absolutely contains more nutritious matter than two pounds of flesh-meat (890), why is it that those who are accustomed to animal food immediately droop and feel weak and languid when flesh-meat is withheld from them? and why is their usual vigour restored when they return to their customary diet?

906. Flesh-meat is more stimulating in proportion to the quantity of nourishment it affords than vegetable food; and (880) every stimulation increases what is called tone. By so much, therefore, as flesh-meat is more stimulating, it gives to those who are accustomed to it a *feeling* of greater strength than vegetable food; and (883), whenever a *less* is substituted for a *more* stimulating diet, a depression succeeds, and as this is removed by a return to the stimulus (882), those who are accustomed to animal food have

found that when they abstain from flesh-meat they feel less energetic, and when they return to it they feel more vigorous ; hence they have inferred that animal food is more nourishing than vegetable food.

907. But if this *experience* proves animal food to be more nourishing than vegetable, it also proves that the stimulants which actually afford no nourishment to the system, are really invigorating to the body (884).

908. As pure stimulants afford no nourishment, and flesh-meat nourishes while it stimulates, the depression experienced from a sudden abandonment of the latter, though less distressing, is generally of greater duration than from abandonment of the former.

909. But as flesh-meat is more stimulating in proportion to the nourishment than vegetable aliment (906), the processes of nutrition in the use of the former are attended with a greater expenditure of vital power (879). The chyme formed from it, the chyle, the blood, and all the fluids elaborated from the blood, are more exciting and cause a greater expenditure in the system (991). Hence in the healthy and robust accustomed to vegetable and water diet, the skin is cooler and the pulse slower than in those on a mixed diet (476).

910. As flesh-meat passes more rapidly through the processes of assimilation than vegetable food (909), it is supposed to be more easily digested by the dyspeptic. But the assimilating processes are to be contemplated as vital, effected by the living organs, and attended with expenditure of the tissues and functional powers (875) ; consequently the ease with which any substance is digested is not determined by time, but by the amount of vital power required. The substance which causes the greatest expenditure in the functional process is the most difficult to digest, whether the time be long or short.

911. Hence, they who subsist on animal food always feel more dull during digestion, and (328), suffer more distress from hunger (882) than they who subsist on a vegetable aliment. This is one reason why they who subsist on well-chosen vegetable diet can endure fatigue and exposure longer without food than they who subsist on flesh-meat.

912. The physiological difference between the two kinds of aliment is greater than is indicated by chemical analysis. Hence, two pounds of good bread will sustain a man accustomed to such diet better than eight pounds of flesh-meat.

913. Russian and Greek labourers will work from twelve to sixteen hours a day on about one pound of coarse bread, with garlics, figs, raisins, apples, or other fruit. Millions in India and China subsist on a few ounces of rice a day each ; and where in other respects correct, they are well nourished.

914. Though the chemical character of the chyle is nearly identical, whatever the substance from which it is elaborated (455), yet the *vital constitution* of the chyle and blood is greatly affected by the quality of the food. When chyle is taken from the living vessels, that elaborated from flesh-meat (126) will putrefy in three or four days ; while that from vegetable aliment will resist the action of inorganic affinities for weeks (456). Blood formed from animal food will putrefy in a shorter time and more rapidly than that formed

from vegetable aliment; and there is always a greater febrile tendency in those who subsist on animal than those who subsist on vegetable food.

XV.

[*Argues that the human body is the highest of material forms, and dilates on the moral power of personal beauty.*]

944. Fashion defines the shapes we worship, however unfriendly to the interests of our nature! The garment is according to fashion, and the body squeezed into it, no matter how much deformity that garment hides. The waist must be reduced, other parts filled out by padding, and human beings tortured into *such* models of elegance. Almost every caprice of fashion is unfavourable to our well-being, calculated to destroy natural symmetry, and make us deformed.

945. It is surprising how rarely bodily symmetry is met with in civic life.

947. Causes acting through generations will degenerate the race, and establish peculiarities which give the appearance of distinct species.

962. The development, symmetry, and growth, as well as natural termination of life, are connected with the conditions of the solids and fluids. (674). Whatever changes the relative conditions impairs the results of the vital economy (680-681). When the solids and fluids are brought into a certain state, the growth ceases, whether the body is fully developed or not; and when this is produced by irritating or too accelerating causes, the results will be imperfect (914).

963. The use of opium and other substances by the mother often deforms the offspring; and vice in early youth often arrests the growth, brings on an untimely age, decrepitude, and death.

964. Animal food cannot be so conducive as vegetable food to the development and symmetry of the body; because, possessing a greater proportion of stimulating power, it (906) more rapidly exhausts the vital organs (909), accelerates the functions of the system, and renders them less perfect (914).

965. The slower the growth of organic bodies, consistently with healthy action, the more complete the vital processes, the more perfect and symmetrical the development. This law extends even to crystals; those formed most slowly are the most perfect and beautiful.

969. Professor Lawrence tells us that "the Laplanders, Samoies, Ostiacs, Tungooses, Burats, and Kamtschadales, in northern Europe and Asia, as well as the Esquimaux in the northern, and the natives of Terra del Fuego in the southern extremity of America, although they live almost entirely on flesh, and that often raw, are the smallest, weakest, and least brave people of the globe."

970. Dr. Lambe also instances the Laplanders; the inhabitants of the Andaman Islands; the Ostiacs; the New Hollanders: the tribes on the coast of Terra del Fuego, &c.

978. If a miracle be admitted in the case of Daniel. it goes more strongly to establish the principles contended for, on divine authority.

979. Dr. Lambe contrasts the natives of Otaheite, the Friendly and Society

Isles ; the NewZealanders ; the Circassians ; the Ricaras ; the Finns ; the Indians of Mexico on the Tobasco River, &c., all of whom subsist chiefly on vegetable food, with the flesh-eating tribes previously mentioned ; the former being in all respects very superior to the latter. A native of the Marquesas, carefully measured, corresponded in every part with the Apollo Belvidere. The food of these people consists of bread-fruit, cocoa-nuts, bananas, yams, battatas, &c., and mostly in a natural state.

985. Taking all flesh-eating nations together, though some whose habits are favourable are comparatively well-formed, as a general average they are small, ill-formed races. And taking all vegetable-eating nations, though many, from their excessive use of narcotics (963), and from other unfavourable circumstances (902), are comparatively small and ill-formed, as a general average they are much better formed races than the flesh-eaters. It is only among those tribes whose habits are temperate, and who subsist on a vegetable diet, that the most perfect specimens of symmetry are found (1030).

XVI.

990. The more stimulating the diet, the more rapidly the changes in the condition of the solids and fluids take place, and the body loses its activity. Hence, fleshmeat is not so conducive to suppleness, grace, &c., as proper vegetable food (909).

[*Mentions several examples of comparative activity among persons subsisting on vegetable food.*]

1003. Among hundreds in the United States who have adopted a vegetable diet, where temperance and general propriety have been observed, there has been experienced a considerable increase of activity.

1004. In regard to bodily strength, two principles are to be considered : the mechanical and the physiological. Some have such a mechanical construction of body as gives them astonishing strength, while their muscles possess no more power of contractility, in a given volume, than those of much less strength.

1006. The physiological element of voluntary power is muscular contractility ; and the degree of contractile power in any muscle depends on (142) the healthiness of its structure. There are certain kinds of diet which, so long as the vital economy can sustain their forcing influence, increase the function of nutrition (499), round out the limbs, and seem to increase the muscular fibre, when in fact the muscular structure is little increased, but a quantity of adipose (498) matter is deposited in the tissue which surrounds every muscle and fibre (170). But such increase of volume is so far from increasing the muscular power, that it necessarily diminishes it.

1011. Flesh-meat (906) being more stimulating than vegetable aliment increases vital action (909), renders the organic structure less perfect, and increases the expenditure of organised substance (914), giving to the muscular tissue less power of contractility, to the nervous tissue less energetic stimulus, and producing blood less adapted to sustain vital action (685).

1014. Vegetable-eating animals are stronger and capable of greater endurance than carnivorous animals. In muscular power the rhinoceros exceeds all animals, eating the limbs of trees, shivering their trunks, and consuming them like grass.

[*Gives instances of strength among ancient Persians, Spartans, Russians, Indians, Chinese, Moors, &c., &c., all living on vegetable food ; also many individual cases.*]

1052. Thomas M'Goodin, in the Callendar factory, Providence, about forty years old (Feb., 1834), small frame, weighs a hundred and thirty pounds, was induced, about 1825, to abandon animal food, and adopt vegetable and water diet. After about seven years, a competition arose in the beetling department, in which the ability to endure protracted effort was severely tried. Two stations requiring the same exertion were occupied several days in succession. M'Goodin took one through the whole time without flagging, while the other was successively occupied by four of the strongest men, all of whom were tired out. The overseer believed M'Goodin would kill every man in the establishment if they were obliged to hold their way till he gave out. M'Goodin also laboured from one to two hours a-day longer than any other man.

1054. It is certain that, all other things being equal, they who subsist on a diet of well-chosen vegetable food and water, possess more muscular power, and are able to perform more labour in a given time, and to labour much longer without rest, than they who subsist either on animal food or a mixed diet.

XVII.

1056. Many seem to think that physicians can take disease out and put health into them, by remedies, and that there is in the remedies themselves a health-giving potency which imparts health to the body.

1057. This leads people to place their dependence on remedies, and to undervalue the highest qualifications of the scientific physician (34). The result is, mankind do not believe that their dietetic and other habits have anything to do with the preservation of health ; in the second place, when diseased, they expect to be cured by medicine, and do not believe that diet can be of importance in promoting their restoration to health.

1061. Medical men have been divided into three schools. First, those who have considered disease to consist in certain conditions of the fluids of the body. This is the foundation of humoral pathology. Their modes of treatment have been pursued with reference to the state of the fluids, aiming to correct the humours.

1062. The second school consider that disease consists in the peculiar condition of the solids; that by the action of disturbing causes the solids are irritated, and derangement of function, inflammation, fevers, change of structure, &c., are induced. They seek to restore health by abstracting irritating causes, and by the exhibition of sedative medicine, or to overcome the unhealthy action of one part by producing irritation in another, on the principle of counter irritation ; and it is upon this principle that accidental cures are effected to which medicines owe their reputation. People oppress their systems till they begin to be affected with disturbed action. These symptoms they mistake for disease itself, and fly to remedies for sour stomachs, dizziness, headache, sore eyes, rheumatism, pain in the breast, side, or back, or for catarrh, cough, cramps, eruption, debility, &c. If the symptoms arise from oppression caused by excessive alimentation, any drug which will evacuate the alimentary cavity and cause depletion will give relief. Or if the symptoms arise from the unhealthy action of some particular organ, the medicine, by rallying the vital forces in reaction, induces a new disease, which, upon the principle of counter irritation, causes a determination from the old to the new point of morbid action, and thus, perhaps, subdues the symptoms and receives the credit of curing the disease. The vital economy will often avail itself of the new action to recover the health of the part affected, yet it is at the expense of injury to other parts. And if the cause which induced the diffi- culty be continued, the result will be, either that the old symptoms will return with increased violence, or other symptoms, modified by the medicine, or arising from the diseased conditions predisposed by the effect of the medi- cine, will take place. But, so that the symptoms are temporarily subdued, the sufferer is deceived into the belief that he is benefited by the medicine, and perseveres in the use of remedies which become the causes of suffering, till he drugs himself to death.

1063. The third school combine the views of the others. They consider that the solids and fluids are both concerned in disease. No doubt the diseased condition and action of the solids produce a morbid state of the fluids, and this reacts upon the solids to aggravate their disease. But healthy chyme is produced by the healthy function of the alimentary canal (320), which can perform this function only while itself in an undisturbed condition. Healthy chyle can only be produced by the healthy function of the lacteals (455). Healthy blood can only be produced by the healthy function of the lacteals, lungs, &c., concerned in the formation of blood (474). Healthy bile can only be produced by the healthy function of the liver ; and so on. Now suppose the chyme, chyle, blood, bile, &c., be unhealthy, is it possible to apply such a remedy as will directly impart health ? There is no way of producing the effect but by the healthy function of the organs. The healthy function of the liver alone can make the bile healthy ; and while the function of the liver is healthy, the bile cannot be unhealthy. If the blood is impure, no medicine can directly purify it. There is no way by which it can be purified, but by the healthy function of the appropriate organs.

1066. The scientific physician is generally able to discover the nature of our disease, and to ascertain what disturbing causes must be removed, and what means employed to restore healthy action, and thus, by assisting nature, relieve the system from disease.

1067. The natural result of all normal operations is health ; and if disease is induced, it is by causes which disturb those operations. Indeed, disease may be said to be an excess of action to resist morbific causes. All the aid nature can receive is the removal of disturbing causes, and she will naturally return to health, unless the constitution has received irreparable injury. Disease is not only induced but is kept up by the continual action of disturbing causes. Hence, chronic disease is kept alive by the constant action of dietetic and other habits.

1068. All medicine is in itself an evil ; its direct effect unfriendly to life (1062). In the present condition of human nature there are cases of disease in which medicine is necessary, yet it is at best a necessary evil, and the physician who assists nature to recover health, with the least use of medicine, deserves our highest respect.

1072. States of the atmosphere have often been exciting causes of disease when there was a predisposition to disease by other causes. The grand sources of disease, however, are the erroneous habits of mankind. By error in regard to food, exercise, rest, cleanliness, over-excitements of the mind, inordinate exercise of the passions, etc., the nervous system is kept in a state of irritation, and the power to withstand the action of pestilence is diminished.

1075. Mere abstinence from animal food, without regard to a proper regimen, will not enable man to withstand the action of foreign morbific causes better than a mixed diet under good regulations. Vegetable food can be made more pernicious than plain animal food in temperate quantities. It is better to subsist on a mixed diet under a good general regimen, than to live on vegetable food badly selected and viciously prepared in the violation of every rule of health. In comparisons of animal and vegetable food, all other things must be equal.

1077. Howard was probably more exposed to pestilential causes than any other human being. In seventeen years he travelled sixty thousand miles for the sole purpose of relieving the distresses of the most wretched. The fatigues, the privations he underwent few could have endured. He often travelled several nights and days in succession without stopping, in weather the most inclement. Heat and cold, rain and snow, in all their extremes, failed alike to stay him for a moment ; whilst plague and pestilence were horrors to which he exposed himself ; visiting the foulest dungeons, filled with malignant infection, spending forty days in a filthy lazaretto, plunging into encampments where plague was committing horrid ravages, and visiting where none of his ·conductors dared to accompany him. Through all this he subsisted on a rigidly abstemious vegetable diet, avoiding all alcholic drinks. He was more successful in treating the plague than any of the physicians. The abstemious diet which he adopted he continued from principle and a conviction of the great advantages which he derived from it. Near the close of his life, he made the following record in his diary : " I am firmly persuaded, as to the health of our bodies, that herbs and fruits will sustain nature in every respect far beyond the best flesh." Yet there is reason to believe that he fell a victim to substituting tea for the sustaining nourishment of food, when his body, by fatigue, cold, wet, and exhaustion was unprepared to resist malignantly noxious agents, and then neglected the early symptoms of disease.

[*Several other examples of the resistance of morbific agents during epidemic fevers and cholera, among persons subsisting on vegetable diet.*]   *

1089. A physician is called to a case of violent delirium ; without inquiring after the cause, he bleeds copiously, rapidly reducing the patient without mitigating the symptoms. Another is called who, ascertaining the cause, an emetic is prescribed, and soon a large quantity of undigested beef and pickled cucumbers is thrown from the stomach, and the symptoms disappear (587).

1090. All practice not based upon investigation of causes more frequently does harm than good. In multitudes of people afflicted for years by diseases induced by the use of alcoholic and narcotic substances, and kept alive by the use of these as medicine, all that was necessary to remove the diseases was to take away their medicine. Individuals suffering under affections of heart and head, and submitted to medical treatment for years without the least relief, have, on taking away their tea and coffee, which were the principal causes of their sufferings, been soon restored to health. I have seen hundreds of dyspeptics who had suffered for years; scores whose symptoms indicated consumption; many afflicted with epileptic fits and spasmodic affections, or asthma, after resisting every kind of medical treatment have yielded to a correct diet and regimen. The diseases had been originated by dietetic errors, and with all their medicine those errors had previously remained unquestioned.

1094. "For those who are extremely broken down with chronic disease," says Dr. Cheyne, "I have found no other relief than a total abstinence from all animal food, and from all sorts of strong and fermented liquors."

1095. In regulating diet the suddenness of any change should correspond with the physiological circumstances of the individual; and *the diseased organ should be made the standard of the ability of the system.* As with the boiler of a steam-engine, he who has diseased lungs or liver, while he has a vigorous stomach, must not regulate his food by his stomach, but by the diseased part. Individuals labouring under chronic disease often indulge in improper food, still contending for the propriety of their habits because " *their stomachs never trouble them.*" Alas! they know not that the stomach is the principal source of their troubles (511).

1096. When a patient has an acute disease, the physician adopts a treatment which reduces his strength, because when the action of the vital powers is diseased the more violent it is, and the sooner will it destroy the diseased parts. But the main difference between acute and chronic disease is in the *degree* of the morbid activity; and if we would not indulge in " a generous diet," when labouring under acute inflammation, lest we destroy life by general fever, with what propriety can we indulge when labouring under chronic inflammation, since this as certainly tends to change of structure as the acute, though with less rapidity, because the morbid activity is less excessive, and with less violence, because the system makes less resistance (1067), but more quietly succumbs (729). The more you nourish a body while diseased action is kept up, the more you increase the disease. The object to be aimed at is to remove diseased action, and then nourish the body as fast as the *feeblest parts* of the system will bear. The regimen may cause a diminution of flesh while the disease remains (1095), but when healthy action takes place, the same will increase the flesh and strength.

1097. Some, after trying medicine and generous living for years, with continual suffering, have adopted vegetable diet and general regimen, and soon experienced alleviation or removal of their disease.

1099. The more slowly living bodies are developed, the longer will be the natural duration of life (678). *Intensive* and *extensive* life are incompatible. "The more slowly man grows," says Hufeland, "the later he attains to maturity and the longer all his powers are in expanding, the longer will be the duration of his life—as the existence of a creature is lengthened in proportion to the time required for expansion" (990), (146). In childhood (674), the proportion of the fluids to the solids is more than ten to one ; as life advances the proportion diminishes, and the solids increase (678). This change may be effected slowly or rapidly, according to the habits of the individual (680), (681).

1100. Alcohol ; narcotics (963), (733) ; improper quantities and qualities of food ; inordinate passions, etc., increase the intensity of life and shorten existence. Hence Hufeland observes : " If you would live long, live moderately and avoid a stimulating, heating diet, such as a great deal of flesh, eggs, chocolate, wine, and spices."

1101. An exclusive vegetable diet, with every other circumstance unfavourable to life, will not sustain human existence so well as a mixed diet, with every other circumstance favourable (1075). The Hindoos subsist mostly on vegetable food ; but (1021) they eat also stimulating spices ; they smoke a composition containing opium, and chew opium, lime, and betel-nut, wrapped up in a sera-leaf of very acrid and pungent qualities. Tobacco, one of the worst narcotics, and arrack are also in common use. They are licentious and inactive, and their climate is by no means favourable to life. Is it strange that such people should afford few instances of longevity ? Yet it is common for the Brahmins, who are temperate, to attain to a hundred years (756).

1103. Great longevity is never found among tribes who subsist principally on animal food. The Patagonians, with a climate and every circumstance except diet favourable to longevity, rarely attain seventy years of age (971).

[*Instances of longevity among vegetable-eating Chinese, Pythagoreans, Essenes, Swiss, Russians ; Bowman, Old Parr, Henry Jenkins, &c.*]

1107. When individuals who have lived to sixty or seventy years on a mixed diet, and experience many infirmities, adopt a well-chosen vegetable diet and good general regimen, they greatly improve and throw off many of their infirmities (1047).

1112. To say nothing of the vegetable-eating millions of Asia, a large majority of the Irish never partake of flesh-meat, and yet Ireland, besides being in such a state of overfulness as to be constantly threatened with want of food, has deluged England and America with her offspring.

1114. The man accustomed to vegetable diet can endure severer cold, or the same degree of cold much longer, than the man accustomed to a flesh diet.

1115. Animal heat is the effect of vital function (489), and the power of the body to regulate its temperature so as to sustain the extremes of heat and cold is greatest when in the most healthy state (986).

1117. No exiles to the wintry region of Siberia endure the severities of the climate better than those accustomed to a vegetable diet.

XVIII.

1126. A correct vegetable diet is more conducive to high sensorial power in the nervous system than flesh meat ; and the senses of touch, taste, smell, hearing, sight, and the intellectual and moral faculties are more perfect.

1128. Predaceous animals, which subsist entirely on flesh, possess powerful senses. In the special senses there is a nice distinction between simple *power* and *discrimination*. A hound may have the power of scenting its game farther than a sheep can smell its food, while the olfactory sense of the sheep may be more nicely discriminating. The first depends on anatomical arrangement, the second on sensorial power. In animals which have the power of scenting their game at a distance the olfactory nerves are larger than in other animals, and ramified over more extensive nasal surfaces ; while in herbivorous animals which require an olfactory sense to discriminate the qualities of substances, the olfactory nerves are smaller and more simple.

1129. The sensorial power even of carnivorous animals is exalted by abstinence from flesh. In preparing hounds for the chase they are trained for at least a fortnight, when all animal food is taken from them, and they are kept upon coarse bread with water, because flesh-eating deadens the sensibility and power of the olfactory nerves and makes the hounds sluggish.

1130. Physiological science proves that a well-ordered vegetable diet is more conducive to the functional power and integrity of the organs of special sense, than a diet which includes any flesh-meat.

1153. It has been a matter of very frequent and extensive observation that those who, having been accustomed to flesh-meat, abandon it and subsist on vegetable diet, experience a great improvement in their special senses—generally much sooner in the smell and taste, than in the sight and hearing. In some cases the sudden substitution of a less for a more stimulating diet will cause a temporary depression (883), and the senses are involved in the general effect, but as soon as the body becomes adapted to the new diet the tone of the system is elevated, and the powers of the special senses improved.

1154. "Not only are the special senses improved by the disuse of flesh, but this improvement," says Dr. Lambe, "pervades every organ and influences every function of the system. There is no organ of the body which, under the use of vegetable food, does not receive a healthy increase of its peculiar sensibility."

[*That vegetable food is most conducive to intellectual vigour, quotes Dr. Lambe, Sir John Sinclair, Franklin, &c., with illustrations.*]

1181. A vast amount of intellectual capability lies undeveloped and kept in inactivity by dietetic habits. Let these habits be changed, and an increase of cheerfulness, sensorial power, and mental activity will be experienced in consequence.

1188. Where there is predisposition to insanity I know of no precaution

G

more sure to prevent its development than a simple vegetable diet, with a correct general regimen.

1189. "J. C.," in 1836, stated to me that insanity had been hereditary in his family ; that he found himself seriously threatened, and began to experience distressing symptoms, when he attended my lectures in 1832, and adopted the system of living recommended. Soon after he found his health improving ; his mental disorder disappeared ; and he had since enjoyed perfect health of body and mind.

XIX.

[Treats of the advantage of unstimulating diet in relation to the moral faculties.]

XX.

1244. *We may maintain* [apparent] *health at the expense of life.* Or, as Hufeland expresses it (1105), "very sound [apparent] health may shorten life ;" *i.e.*, we may maintain health to old age in spite of habits which hasten the consumption of life and shorten our existence. For (1092) *intensive* and *extensive* life are incompatible, and flesh-meat causes more vital intensiveness than vegetable food (909). Apparent health, therefore, is not a proof that our habits are conducive to longevity.

1245. "I am now too far advanced in life to make any changes in my habits," said a gentleman, about seventy, of portly appearance, and apparent good health. He had a large frame, florid complexion, and was strictly temperate. "I have the best evidence that my habits have been very salutary, for I am in the enjoyment of uncommon health, and during life have not been so much indisposed as to keep my house for a single day." "Indeed, sir," was the reply, "that may be your misfortune. Judging from the soundness of your constitution, you are now little past the meridian of life, and the health of which you boast may have served to blind you to errors which may have robbed you of half your natural existence. Not one human being in a million dies a natural death. If a man is shot or poisoned, we say he dies a violent death ; but if he is ill, attended by physicians, and dies, we say he dies a natural death. Now this is an abuse of language ; the death in the latter case is as truly violent as if he had been shot. Whether a man takes arsenic and kills himself, or by small doses, or other means however common, gradually destroys life, he equally dies a violent death (1096). He only dies a natural death who so obeys the laws of his nature as neither by irritation nor intensity to waste his energies, but slowly passes through the changes of his system to old age and falls asleep in the exhaustion of vitality."

1246. The gentleman was soon after taken ill, and died, having requested that his body might be opened. And never was found disease more extensive than in this case. The stomach and intestinal canal presented one general mass of disease, which indicated a progress of several years, the result of causes operating by imperceptible degrees.

1247. The cause of his death was the habitual over-working of organs, which a vigorous constitution had sustained (729), though unable to manifest those symptoms which would have enabled him to take precautions, and therefore it proceeded to his destruction without being suspected.

1249. Butchers are referred to as evincing the healthy effect of a free use of flesh. But there is less meat consumed by butchers than is supposed. As a class they do not consume more than others, and many of them eat less; whilst they eat none but the best. Nevertheless there is more indisposition among butchers than is supposed, and the diseases are generally violent and apt to terminate fatally. The robust appearance of butchers is attributable to their habits of active employment in the open air.

1250. It is a common notion that a florid countenance is a sign of good health, and a pale complexion an indication of poor health. But it is far from true that a ruddy countenance is always the index of health or long life. "Too much ruddiness in youth," says Hufeland, "is seldom a sign of longe-vity." At all periods it indicates that state in which, either from disease or intensity, the vital expenditure is too rapid. The clear complexion in which the red and white is so delicately blended as to produce a soft flesh-colour, varying from a deeper to a paler hue according as the individual is accustomed to exercise in the open air, or to sedentary habits, is the best index of health most favourable to length of days.

1259. The dietetic regulations of Moses tolerate the use of flesh on the same principle that he suffered them to put away their wives. The Mosaic dis-pensation aimed rather to restrict than to encourage the use of this food, and his regulations were designed to restrain as much as possible to the least objectionable kinds.

1263. Moses proclaimed it as "a perpetual statute for their generations, throughout all their dwellings, that they should eat no manner of fat, of ox, nor of sheep, nor of goat nor of any other beast."

1269. Fat meats and animal oils debilitate the digestive organs, and induce a chronic morbid irritability. The character of the disease they cause varies according to the peculiar predisposition and habits of individuals. It may take the form of dyspepsy, liver complaint, chronic diarrhœa, pulmonary consumption, sick-headache, eruptions of the skin, erysipelas, etc. In hot climates the injurious effects of oily food are more powerfully felt than in cold climates; hence, though it may be tolerated with *apparent* safety in the latter, it must be avoided in the former.

1279. If the human race will eat flesh-meat, the best mode of cooking it is to roast, broil, or boil it. Roasting before a fire, turned till moderately done, is the best manner of cooking. Boiling renders it less stimulating and also less nourishing. Stewing flesh is a more objectionable mode; and frying in fat is the most pernicious manner in which it can be prepared. It is enough to break down the digestive powers.

1281. Every kind of concentrated aliment is injurious (738—745). Flesh broths consist of water holding in solution some of the nutrient principles in a concentrated form. When swallowed, the first duty which the stomach performs is to take up (440, 442) the water while the concentrated animal matter is retained to be digested and passed into the intestinal tube; and as there has been no mastication of this food, when the water is absorbed the concentrated animal matter is left more dry than food received in a solid form and masticated. Aliment, when properly masticated, excites more copious secretion of the gastric juice, and a more vigorous action of the muscular tissue of the stomach. Flesh broths, therefore, irritate and debilitate the digestive organs, and should be avoided.

1282. Salted flesh and fish are less easily digested and less nourishing than fresh. Salt is an indigestible substance, and when it has penetrated animal substances so as to preserve them from putrefaction, it renders them more difficult of digestion, and consequently causes irritation to the digestive organs.

1283. Flesh and fish that are both salted and smoked are yet more difficult of digestion. Yet it is not uncommon to see upon the table of invalids salted and smoked fish, saturated with butter, and perhaps dressed with mustard and pepper. Such a dish is enough to give a hyena a fit of dyspepsy.

1284. Gravies containing oily matter, whether dripping or butter, are exceedingly mischievous. Execrable compounds, more fit for the soap-boiler's vat than the human stomach! It would not be easy to measure the evil which these vile dishes cause. They are abominable preparations, and ought to be regarded with deep abhorrence.

1285. Concerning the use of BUTTER, it is remarkable that nearly all who have written on human aliment have agreed in considering this favourite article as objectionable. Dr. Beaumont's experiments (431) prove that butter in the stomach "becomes a fluid oil, and floats upon the top of the chymous mass, retaining its oily character till all the other contents of the gastric cavity are chymified and emptied into the duodenum" (338). It is, therefore, established that butter is better avoided.

1289. CHEESE, in the stomachs of dyspeptics, is a difficult thing to manage ; but robust labouring men are able to digest it in small quantities, without experiencing immediate inconvenience. Rich old cheese, sought after by epicures, is digested with difficulty, causes much irritation, and not un-frequently produces eruptions or inflamed pustules of the mucous membrane. The curd made by the Germans, called pot-cheese, is the least unwholesome.

1290. MILK has been praised as one of the most wholesome kinds of food. Mr. Riley informs us that the Arabs live two or three hundred years, in excellent health, exclusively on the milk of their camels (779). Milk is the natural diet for children, and experience has proved that it is a nourishing food in every situation. For those who are labouring under disease, for the delicate and feeble, the young and the sedentary, a milk and vegetable diet is far better than a flesh and vegetable diet. Nevertheless eight years of extensive experiment and observation have shaken my preconceived opinions concerning milk as human food.

1291. The testimony of hundreds affirms that they do best when they confine themselves to a diet of vegetable food and water. Dyspeptics and invalids, and farmers, mechanics, etc., whose labours are severe, all declare that they feel more vigorous when they abstain from milk and subsist exclusively on vegetable food and water.

1292. The alimentary organs of children are in a condition requiring liquid food, and milk is adapted to their wants. As they grow older, however, new organs are developed (324) adapted to new functions and kinds of aliment ; simultaneously with the development of the teeth correspondent changes take place in the physiological properties and powers of the digestive organs fitted for more solid aliment.

1294. If an animal receives any poisonous substance during lactation, the milk is affected by it. If two cows, the one nursing a calf, and the other giving no milk, receive poison sufficient to cause death, the latter cow will die, while the calf of the former will be killed and the mother escape. In this way infants have been distressed, thrown into convulsions, and even killed by substances swallowed by their mothers ; and in this way thousands have been made seriously ill, and many killed, by poisonous substances which cows have eaten.

1295. But milk is more frequently rendered unwholesome than actually poisonous, for everything that affects the health of the cow affects the milk.

1296. The best milk can only be procured from healthy cows which run at large and crop their food from a pure soil, and, if housed, are kept in clean, well-ventilated stables, curried, cleaned, supplied with pure water, and suffered to take regular exercise in the open air (1286).

1297. Cream, when sweet, is soluble in water, and mixes with the fluids of the mouth and stomach ; therefore, if free from deleterious properties (1294—1296), is far less objectionable than butter. It may be used instead of butter in a variety of ways, if one must be used. The butter spoken of in the Scriptures, in connection with honey, etc., was probably cream.

1298. Eggs are somewhat more animalised than milk, and perhaps rather more exciting to the system. Yet when fresh, if taken raw or slightly cooked, without the use of oily matter, they are not difficult of digestion. But when so much cooked as to become hard they require a vigorous stomach to digest them. All said concerning milk is (1290—1293) applicable to eggs.

XXI.

1306. In the climate most natural to man (1239,) his physiological interests would be best sustained by those vegetable products which require no cooking (760). But as man migrates and becomes acclimated, where he finds it necessary to subsist on different vegetable substances, he may also find it necessary to prepare some of these.

1307. Every means substituted for the natural use of the teeth tends to destroy their power. Every artificial means employed for the regulation of the temperature of the body diminishes its natural power to regulate its own temperature (490). If our feet are cold, and we by walking, dancing, &c., increase in a healthy manner the calorific function of the feet, we invigorate the parts, compatibly with the general interests ; but if we warm our feet by fire, we diminish their natural power to regulate their own temperature. This, illustrates the effects of all other artificial means on the physiological powers. (418).

1308. All artificial preparations of food are in some degree detrimental to our physiological and psychological interests (725). Yet as man may be under the necessity of subsisting on substances less wholesome in their natural state than when prepared by fire, the evil by cooking would be less than that which it would prevent, and in effect a relative good.

1310. If man were to subsist on alimentary substances in their natural state, he would be obliged to use his teeth (709), and not only preserve them from decay (713) but mix his food with the solvent fluid of his mouth and prepare it for the action of the stomach (426); by the same means he would be made to swallow his food slowly, as the welfare of the stomach (429) requires (717).

1311. Again, he would never suffer from the improper temperature of his food (490). Hot substances destroy the teeth (714), debilitate the stomach, and diminish gustatory enjoyment. By abstinence from hot things, also, diseases of the throat, lungs, &c., would be less numerous and frequent.

1312. Again, if man were to subsist on food in a natural state, he would never suffer from concentrated aliment. Nature produces nothing which is purely a concentrated nutrient principle; and the body (683, 757) is organised with reference to this state of things; and hence (751) a due proportion of innutritious matter is as important to health as nutritious matter.

1316. Finally, if man subsisted on uncooked food, the integrity of his appetite (757), his thorough mastication (717), and simple meal, would serve to prevent *over-eating*, and save him from one of the most destructive causes operating in civic life. For excessive alimentation is the cause of more disease than anything else which affects his existence.

1329. Coarse unleavened bread is one of the least removes from the natural state of food, and best adapted to fulfil the laws of constitution and relation (1310, *et seq.*).

1330. "In Scotland", says Dr. Cullen, "nine-tenths of the lower class live upon unfermented bread and farinacea in other forms, and there are not a more healthy people anywhere to be found."

1331. If two portions of wheat-meal be made, one into unleavened the other into leavened bread, and both eaten warm from the oven, the leavened will prove more difficult to digest than the unleavened.

1332. Wheat is decidedly the best material for making raised bread.

1338. Bread is richer if the grain be ground but a short time before it is cooked. The best way is to purchase new wheat, and store where it will be kept dry; and, as needed, wash it in two or three waters, and spread on a drying table, considerably inclined, so that the water will run off. Being thinly spread in a good drying day, it will be sufficiently dry in a few hours for grinding.

1345. Bread made of superfine flour is less wholesome than that made of meal, which contains all the natural properties of the grain (744, 751). All concentrated forms of food are unfriendly to the physiological interests of our bodies (739). The use of superfine flour bread is among the causes of numerous difficulties. Costiveness, even after an obstinate continuance of years, disappears in a short time after coarse bread has been substituted for that made of fine flour.

1346. Everything nature provides for food consists of certain proportions of nutritious and innutritious matter; and the latter is as essential to the functional integrity of our organs as the former to the sustenance of the body (1312).

1348. Coarse bread is as excellent a remedy for chronic diarrhœa as for chronic constipation.

1349. Coarse bread *seems* to increase the disease for a short time, and then gradually restores healthy action. The mucilage of bran is most soothing to the mucous membrane.

1350. Chronic constipation and chronic diarrhœa both spring from the same root. Where the vigour of the alimentary canal is considerable, continued irritation, resulting in debility, will produce constipation; and this cause, operating for some time, will induce such irritability as is attended with diarrhœa; and when this vigour is less, diarrhœa is more readily induced.

[*Several examples of the advantages of coarse bread in imparting strength*, e.g., *Spartans, Romans, Germans, French, and English, are given on the authority of Hippocrates, Pliny, Tryon, Steuben, Peters, Prior, Rees, &c.*]

1360. According to Professor Thomson, one pound of wheat-meal contains ten ounces of farina, three ounces of bran, six drachms of gluten, and two drachms of sugar. The farina is the principal nourishing property; the saccharine matter is also nutrient; but in making bread it serves mainly, by its vinous fermentation, to produce the gas by which the dough is raised. The gluten is likewise nutrient, but principally serves, by its cohesiveness, to prevent the air formed by fermentation from escaping; and the gas thus retained inflates the dough and makes it light. The mucilaginous bran not only adds to the nutritiousness of the bread, but serves to increase its digestibility.

1361. The next thing necessary is good yeast, to produce the vinous fermentation of the sugar. However light that bread may be made with brewers' yeast, I have rarely seen any in which I could not detect disagreeable properties. There are various ways of making domestic yeast. Put into one gallon of water a double handful of hops; boil twenty minutes; strain off while scalding hot; stir in meal till it becomes a thick batter, so that it will hardly pour; let it stand till blood warm; add a pint of yeast; stir it well, and let it stand at a temperature of seventy degrees, till it becomes light, and then it is fit for use. Or if it is desired to keep a portion, let it become cool, then cork it tight, and place where it will keep cool. It may be preserved twelve days, and even longer.

1363. Fermentation cannot go on when the temperature is below thirty degrees; it proceeds slowly at fifty degrees, moderately at sixty, rapidly at seventy, and very rapidly at eighty degrees. If it is desired to have the dough stand several hours before it is baked, it should be kept at a temperature of fifty degrees. But in the ordinary way a temperature of from sixty to seventy degrees is as near right as it can be made.

1366. If fermentation be permitted to go beyond the sugar, and act on the mucilage and starch, and produce acidity, the excellence of the bread is in some degree destroyed. The acid may be neutralised by soda, so that the bread shall not be sour ; but still something of the natural flavour of the bread is gone, and it is not possible to restore it. When the dough is raised enough to mould it into the loaf, if it is found to be in any degree acid, a solution of soda is worked in so as just to neutralise the acid, and no more. This is better than to have sour bread, yet bread made in this way is only second best. Happy are those who can make light, sweet bread without suffering the least acetous fermentation to take place, and employing soda.

1369. Take meal necessary for the bread desired, and having made a hollow, turn in yeast as experience shall deem requisite [*about a teacupful to a peck— depending on its liveliness*]; add water at blood heat necessary to form the meal into dough of proper consistency.

1370. Good bread cannot be made by merely stirring the meal, yeast, and water together into dough, and suffering it to ferment with little kneading. Bread made in this manner, if it is not full of cavities, surrounded by solid parts, is full of cells, and the bread has a glutinous appearance, showing that it has not been mixed, and the yeast has acted unequally.

1371. If the yeast be so diffused and the dough be of such a consistency and temperature as not to admit of too rapid fermentation, then each portion of saccharine matter in fermentation will form its little cell about the size of a pin's head, and smaller ; and this so nearly at the same time that the whole will be made light before the acetous fermentation takes place in any part. And then, properly baked, it will make delicious bread.

1373. It should be kneaded till it becomes flaky.

1374. Wheat-meal swells considerably, and therefore the dough should not be made quite so stiff as that made of flour ; and when it is raised, if it is found too soft to mould, let a little more be added.

1375. When thoroughly kneaded cover the dough with a napkin and a light woollen blanket, where the temperature will be sixty degrees, till it becomes light. But as it is impossible to regulate your yeast, the temperature, &c., as to secure at all times precisely the same results, it is necessary that the moment be seized to mould the loaf, and get it into the oven just when it is as light as it can be made before the acetous fermentation commences. If there should be acidity in the dough, take carbonate of soda, and dissolve in warm water, and work in just enough to neutralise the acid. Dip the fingers into the solution and thrust them into the dough in every part, so as to get in just enough to neutralise the acid, and not a particle more. Dough made of wheat-meal will become sour sooner than that made of fine flour.

1376. The baking requires as much judgment as any part of bread-making. If the oven is too hot, the bread will burn on the outside before it is done ; if too cold , the bread will be heavy, raw, and sour. If the heat is greater below than above, the bottom will burn before the top is done ; or if the heat is greater above than below, the top of the loaf will burn before the bottom is done. Dough made of meal requires a hotter oven than that made of flour, and needs to remain in longer.

1379. If the crust should be too dry and crispy, you can remedy this by throwing a cloth over it for a short time, when it comes from the oven. Let the bread stand on an airy shelf till it becomes cool, and when twenty-four hours old it is fit for use.

[*Strongly recommends the mother of every family to make her own bread.*]

1394. Rye, raised on a sandy soil, will make excellent bread ; also when mixed with Indian meal.

1395. There are various ways of preparing Indian meal bread in such a manner as to render it very wholesome.

1396. Barley, oats, rice, arrow-root, tapioca, sago, peas, beans, chestnuts, millet, buckwheat, potatoes, etc., may also, by mixing them with a portion of wheat or rye flour, be manufactured into bread.

1397. In making bread from Indian meal and other substances containing little gluten, yeast is rarely used, but sour milk, or buttermilk and soda. Take sour milk and stir meal into it till a thin batter is formed ; dissolve soda, and stir that into the batter, and then hastily add meal till the batter is brought to the consistency desired. If, instead of milk, tartaric acid is used, the bread will be equally light, the batter being first made with a solution of soda, and then the solution of acid stirred in.

1399. Perfect bread-making is the perfection of cooking ; but compounds of flour and butter or lard, sugar, eggs and spices, etc., comprehended by the term " pastry," are among the most pernicious articles of food, doing incomparably more mischief than simply prepared flesh meat (1075). For the mixing of any kind of animal fat with vegetable substance in the making of puddings, cakes, &c., is more irritating to the stomach than almost any food eaten by civilised man (1287).

1400. Cream, not more than twelve hours from the cow (1297), is far less objectionable than butter or other animal fat. Therefore, if shortening *must* be used in the preparation of pastry, cream is vastly preferable.

1401. A small quantity of new milk or cream, or both together, may also be used in making toast with comparatively little objection.

1402. Rice, wheat, Indian corn, &c., may be converted into puddings in a simple and wholesome manner. Custards made of eggs (1298), milk, and sugar, slightly cooked, are comparatively innocent for occasional use. Some make pie-crust by employing boiled and finely-mashed potatoes for shortening.

1405. Beans, peas, potatoes, beet, carrots, parsnips, turnips, pumpkins, squashes, cabbage, &c., are among the vegetables which at most require simple boiling, roasting, or baking. Cabbage, radishes, cucumbers, lettuce, and other salads are managed with ease by those who subsist wholly on vegetable food properly prepared, and abstain from stimulating substances.

1406. But, besides bread, fruit is the most appropriate food of man (770). Apples, pears, peaches, plums, cherries, grapes, strawberries, raspberries, blackberries, whortleberries, gooseberries, water-melons, musk-melons, &c., may be eaten with or without bread, when ripe, without any preparation. Besides these may be preserved, as substitutes for fruit in its natural state. Sweet apples, ground, and the juice filtered through washed sea-sand and pulverised charcoal, and evaporated over a slow fire, till the juice becomes a thick syrup ; and then mildly acid apples, divested of the skin, put into this syrup, till cooked through, will produce sauce which will serve with bread. Peaches, strawberries, &c., may be preserved in the same manner.

1408. But fruit should be eaten as food, not as mere pastime ; it should be eaten at the table, as portion of the regular meal ; but sparingly at the third meal, especially if taken late. All cooked food impairs the power of the stomach to digest uncooked substances, therefore, so long as we are accustomed to cooked food, we must be careful in regard to the times when we eat fruits in their natural state. Hence, so long as we are accustomed to cooked food, the stomach will always digest fruit in its natural state better in the early than the latter part of the day.

1410. In conclusion, those who *will* eat flesh should use but a small quantity of the healthy lean fibre (1271) once a day (1279), with good bread, and one or two kinds of vegetables, simply prepared ; but while they continue to eat flesh, let them be careful how they indulge in fruits and vegetables in their natural state (1299) ; while they who subsist wholly on vegetable food may enjoy every succulent fruit and vegetable eaten as a portion of the regular meal. The vegetable eater also can prepare many green vegetables, as peas, beans, and other products of the garden, which, although far from being perfectly adapted to his physiological interests, yet, when (1405) eaten plain, are comparatively harmless, and give variety.

XXII.

1418. The greatest well-being of the human system can only be secured by physiological regularity. Indeed, when observed, it will enable the system to endure evils often for a length of time. Thus, to the use of tobacco, opium, alcohol, arsenic, or any other poison, taken in the same quantity at regular periods, it is surprising how the system will accommodate itself (728), and work on with little apparent inconvenience for years. But the same poison, at irregular times and quantities, will far more disturb the system.

1421. In health, hunger will recur with regularity, as an indication of the alimentary wants. But when the habits are irregular, and the periodicity of the vital actions disturbed, the recurrence of the sense of hunger will be commensurably affected.

1422. If an individual eat three meals of vegetable food in about that quantity which the alimentary wants demand, hunger will recur at his regular periods. But if he take more than the wants require, or omit exercise, hunger will not recur at his next stated period ; and if he eat at that time, he will oppress the stomach, and by continuing such transgressions he will bring on a preternatural appetite, which will never be satisfied with such quantity as the system can dispose of without oppression.

1423. If flesh be eaten, all these effects will be more distinct (909). And if stimulants are added, the morbid craving will be still more imperious.

1424. This is a beautiful illustration of the systematic regularity of the physiological operations of our organic economy. The vegetable-eater loses a meal with indifference, fasts twenty-four hours with little diminution of strength, and goes without food several days without suffering intolerable distress. The flesh-eater suffers from fasting (911), and experiences a more rapid decline of muscular power.

1425. Violent excitement of the mind (1414) will instantly destroy hunger ; alcoholic and narcotic stimulants will have the same effect. The Mahomedans and Jews generally make a free use of opium, tobacco, coffee, &c., during their long fasts. In certain individuals a glass of wine or a little brandy and water will serve to excite an appetite ; while a more powerful stimulation will produce the contrary effect ; and in all cases the use of such means impairs the functional power of the stomach.

1426. If the customary hour pass without eating, the sense of hunger will die away ; hence, after our meal-time has passed without taking food, and hunger has subsided, if we eat a hearty meal, the stomach will be oppressed and irritated.

1427. Habitual over-eating causes irritation and debility of the stomach, brings on disease, and generally cuts off life at an early period.

1428. All dietetic error, by which the nerves are irritated, increases the unhealthy despotism of the sense of hunger, and renders it a dangerous guide in regard to times of eating and quantity of food.

1432. Unstimulating, vegetable food passes through the stomach slowly ; while flesh-meat (910) passes rapidly, and leaves the organ more exhausted ; consequently the stomach requires a longer time to rest after the digestion of flesh than after farinaceous food. Yet as flesh is more stimulating in proportion to the nourishment it affords, hunger returns at shorter periods, and the flesh-eater can take his meals more frequently than the vegetable-eater, without inconvenience to his digestive organs in particular ; but the increased action of his vital economy will wear out his constitution in a shorter time (915).

1433. As a rule, when a meal is taken, the stomach cannot perform its function, and have sufficient time to rest, in less than *six hours*. Man violates this rule, and experiences the bitter consequences.

1435. Many have been accustomed to take but two meals a day ; as was the habit of some of the wisest philosophers. Socrates taught his disciples that they who ate more than twice a day were barbarians. It was the custom of the most civilised in Greece and Rome to take a light meal in the forepart of the day, and the principal meal or supper near the close of the afternoon ; and from supper till the hour of sleep was devoted to relaxation and amusement.

1436. This is far more conducive to health than our custom of crowding everything ; compelling the digestive organs, the voluntary muscles, and the brain, all to perform their functions at the same time, and thus embarrass the whole. It is better to eat but two meals a day, than either to eat more frequently than once in six hours, or to hurry from the active employments to our meals, and from our meals back to our employments ; particularly those attended with exercise of the mind (303, 510).

1437. Merchants and others, whose labours are more mental than physical, would gain in every respect if they would breakfast at eight o'clock, close business at three, take their principal meal at four, and devote the remainder of the evening to relaxation.

1438. Let them accustom themselves to farinaceous substances and fruits ; they will find they can go from their eight o'clock breakfast to their four o'clock supper with less "sinking," and perform the duties of the day with less fatigue.

1439. Others, whose employments draw more on the muscular than the sensorial powers, can take more food, and the meals nearer together ; but ought not to eat more frequently than once in six hours ; and then will be more likely to take too much than too little.

1440. If we rise at four, breakfast at six, dine at twelve, and sup at six, it would probably be best for us—if our habits are active—to take three meals a day ; be better to take three meals six hours apart, than the same quantity at two meals eight hours apart.

1447. If obliged to pass our regular meal-time without food till hunger has subsided, it is better to defer eating till the next regular meal-time arrives. But we ought not to make up for the one meal lost, by eating sufficient for two meals at once.

1448. When a meal is lost, the next should not be more full, but rather lighter ; and then the occasional loss of a meal will perhaps prove beneficial, or at least not injurious.

1452. If we experience acidity and other symptoms, caused by eating too often, too fast, and too much, the safest remedy is to lose a meal, or perhaps fast a day, and then return to the regular meals more guardedly, making them lighter at first ; for a fast should never be broken by a very full meal ; but the first one, two, or three meals, in proportion to the duration of the fast, should be lighter than usual.

XXIII.

1468. During growth, the function of nutrition is necessarily somewhat in excess of decomposition ; yet even then the relative activity of the processes is determined according to fixed laws, so that no considerable deviation can take place without injury. When the constitution is vigorous, excessive nutrition may take place without distressing symptoms ; and the individual may be regarded as the personification of health, while his life runs close to the line of active disease (639).

1469. After the body has ceased to grow, there must be a balance of action between the great process of composition and decomposition, of incorporation and elimination ; or the system must suffer.

1472. The fund of life (877) with which every human being comes into existence can be squandered in one-tenth of the time it might last. All vital action is attended with waste (376), and draws from the fund of life ; therefore all *intensity* of vital action (1099) increases expenditure and abbreviates life.

1473. Millions perish by disease from excessive alimentation, &c., where one is able to maintain health under such action till he dies from exhaustion.

1474. Few come into existence with all their organs equally developed. There is in almost every one some hereditary taint or predisposition to disease, but the power of the vital economy corresponds not with the vigour of the strongest organ, but with the weakest. Thus, if an individual has a vigorous stomach and weak lungs, the power to maintain health under excessive alimentation is not equal to the ability of his stomach, but to that of his lungs ; and if he goes beyond, he will break down his lungs and his life (511).

1478. When (1474) the organs are not equally powerful, but some part is constitutionally weak, habitually excessive alimentation will break down the organ naturally most feeble, and develop its predisposition into active disease ; and then the standard of excess, instead of being more than the system requires, is more than the diseased organ can bear (1095).

1479. In all countries where aliment is abundant, gluttony is decidedly the greatest source of suffering and premature death. " Excess in *drinking*," said Hippocrates, " is almost as bad as excess in *eating*." Intoxicating liquors even have caused less disease and untimely death than errors in the *quantity* and quality of food ! A drunkard *sometimes* reaches old age ; a glutton *never* (1316).

1483. *A correct quantity of a less wholesome aliment is better than an excessively small or an excessively large quantity of more wholesome food.*

1486. The only rule as to quantity is : Let every one consider that excessive alimentation is one of the greatest sources of evil (1479) ; that he has a continual tendency to this excess (1480) ; and, therefore, *should restrain himself to the smallest quantity which he finds will meet the alimentary wants of his system, knowing that more than this is evil ! There cannot be a blinder guide than appetite, for the active labourer cannot eat artificially prepared food till his appetite is perfectly satisfied, without experiencing evils from excessive alimentation!* If this is true of the robust, to a much greater extent it is of the sedentary, studious, and feeble.

1488. It will often happen that a regimen under which an individual will feel uncomfortable for a while, and lose in weight, will, after his system has become accustomed to it, remove all uncomfortable feelings, restore his weight, and greatly improve his health.

1489. In some cases of disease it will be necessary to limit the invalid to the smallest quantity that will prevent starvation. " The more you nourish a diseased body," said Hippocrates, " the worse you make it." Yet when such a retrenchment is first commenced, the patient may feel exceedingly uncomfortable, and imagine all his symptoms are becoming more violent.

1490. If an individual finds that he has indulged to excess, so far as to have brought on indigestion or (1452), acidity, headache, &c., let him lose a meal, or fast a day, and after such fast return to his usual meals with caution, eating lightly for a day or two ; with proper exercise, he will throw off every unpleasant symptom.

1496. Man requires less food in old age than in the meridian of life, and it is more essential to his health that his food should be simple. Nothing can be more false than the abominable proverb that "*wine is the old man's milk.*" The old man has less power to resist and repair its deleterious effects ; hence, if a man has used it ever so long, when he begins to approach old age, if he would prolong his life and the possession of his faculties, he must abandon every intoxicating drink, and with regularity confine himself to a plain vegetable diet, diminishing his quantity as the powers of his body decline. His will then be "a green old age," healthful, intelligent, cheerful, and capable of intellectual enjoyment to the last (678.); and, when his fund of life is expended, he will expire like one who falls asleep.

1502. Dietetic changes should take place gradually ; not that there is really danger in changing suddenly from a worse to a better diet, but the uncomfortable feelings which attend sudden changes are such as are certain to drive people back to their old habits. Those disposed to conform to the principles herein advanced, should examine the way, and proceed wisely. Vegetable diet causes no rapturous excitement ; water produces no transports. But the encouragements are health, a cheerful mind, and clear intellectual powers. No one has made a fair beginning of this experiment in less than one year, and five years' conformity is the shortest time that can be considered a fair trial of the system.

1511. If the habits of man were natural, he would rarely experience thirst, and fruits and vegetables would afford all the aqueous matter his vital economy requires (442). So that the system would be saved from improper quantities and qualities of fluid, and the sense of thirst would never become depraved. Many have so regulated their habits as to be able to live without taking any kind of drink for six months ; and have found their health more perfect than when they drank even water.

1513. The physiological necessity for a supply of aqueous matter is the expenditure of the lungs, perspiration, &c.

1515. Copious perspiration is debilitating, and strength is diminished by it. The labouring man, while actively employed, should have only a pleasant moisture on the skin ; and this would rarely cause such exhaustion of serum as to require a copious supply of water. Such a man labours with far less fatigue than he who drinks much and perspires much.

1519. The more exciting the food the more frequent will be the thirst ; hence they who eat flesh (809) are more thirsty than they who subsist on vegetable food. Any preternatural heat in the alimentary canal will superinduce thirst. Animal fats or oils tend to produce gastric irritation and thirst (1268), especially when mixed, as in pastry, &c. If salt, pepper, mustard (733) are used, irritation and thirst will be caused ; and intoxicating drinks will render thirst still more irresistible.

1525. Every family that uses rain or river water should be furnished with a filter. Gravel, sand, and charcoal, will be far better than none. But they are wisest who so live as to require little drink of any kind.

1526. If food, with little mastication, is continually washed down with some kind of drink, digestion, instead of commencing, as it ought, will be delayed till the absorbents can remove the fluid and bring the food into a consistence proper for the action of the gastric juice (1281) ; and now the food, instead of being mixed with saliva (426) and gastric juice, as it came into the stomach (429), lies in an oppressive mass, and the already wearied organ must secrete sufficient solvent fluid to digest it.

1527. If water with food is the cause of functional debility, much more objectionable is hot drink (1311) ; everything taken at a high temperature is relaxing. The teeth are injured by hot drinks (714) ; the throat and stomach are debilitated by them ; and if we use tea, coffee, wine, &c., the mischievous effects are greater. (1528.) Drink, then, should not be taken with the food. It is better, if one is thirsty, to take a draught of water thirty minutes before eating, or four hours after.

1531. In a healthy state, the stomach appreciates *the quality of the stimulus* (286, 726, 727, 950) ; but improper substances so deprave its sensibilities that it *can only appreciate the degree of stimulation* (728). Thus, if tobacco is introduced, its poisonous property is perceived, and alarm promptly given (225, 300, 950) ; but if a very small portion at first, little alarm will be given, and the stomach will keep its troubles to itself. (1532.) If no more is introduced, the organ will soon recover. But if a larger quantity is taken, the stomach, having less power to perceive its properties, will give no more alarm than with the less quantity ; and if this be followed up, gradually increasing the tobacco, the stomach will be no longer able to perceive the quality, and only appreciate the degree of stimulation (728.) If now the tobacco be withheld, the consequence will be a depression corresponding with the depravity (228.) (1533.) The depraved stomach, however, craves its accustomed stimulus, and if tobacco be again introduced, its tone is restored. Thus man is brought to the belief that tobacco is conducive to his comfort, and confirmed in his opinion by—*his own experience.*

1534. This reasoning applies to all other stimulants (879). As they increase vital action they cause expenditure (376) in excess of replenishment (881) ; and the consequence is a commensurate physiological depression, or " indirect debility."

(1536. By over exertion or dietetic errors (510), the body is disturbed, and depression produced. He does not suspect that his disquietude is caused by the substances he uses. He only knows from his *experience* (37) that whenever he feels depressed those substances afford him relief, and he therefore believes them to be salutary.

1539. While stimulation produced by noxious substances is identified (1533) with that produced by appropriate stimuli, giving a sense of enjoyment (1535), their physiological action is very different. Natural stimuli (305) excite the parts, and increase functional energy. But the action caused by substances used purely for their stimulating effect, is the action of resistance (300), or vital reaction (950), which is set up to expel the disturbing cause. This stimulation, though it gives the feeling of strength while it lasts (880), never increases the functional energy of any organ concerned in nutrition, but diminishes the power of those organs.

1542. Salt affords no nourishment ; it is indigestible ; and when taken is eliminated through the kidneys, skin, &c., as an unassimilated mineral substance ;

its acrid quality is offensive to the organs, causing resistance (*this vital reaction constitutes the only stimulation ever produced by salt*); its use is, therefore, attended with irritation, followed by indirect debility ; consequently it tends to produce chronic debility in the stomach, intestines, &c. It never promotes digestion, but is unfavourable to all the vital changes (1282.) Lastly, salt diminishes gustatory enjoyment (701). Incredible as this may appear, every one may demonstrate its truth by three months' fair experiment.

1543. Some animals, such as the deer, when diseased by worms, or bots, will instinctively go in pursuit of salt, not as food, but as medicine, and never for any other purpose. Sailors, when confined to salted food, become afflicted with scurvy. And there is reason to conclude that salt is concerned in the production of cancer, and that it serves to aggravate every species of disease.

1546. Seasonings, such as mustard, pepper, ginger, &c., are mischievous in their effects on the alimentary organs (1534), and retard digestion.

1549. The characteristic of all narcotics is their life-destroying property. But when the system (1532) has been depraved, their stimulation is attended with a pleasurable feeling (1533, 1535), which leads to confidence in their salutary nature. There is not a poison to which the body cannot become accustomed. Arsenic may be taken as freely as salt, and with as little evidence of its poisonous character ; and even prussic acid may be gradually brought to act upon the system till it can be used as a means of exhilaration.

1552. Tobacco is one of the most powerful poisons (1534), yet an appetite for this filthy weed is more difficult to overcome than almost any other (768). Opium is essentially like tobacco, except that opium, by being taken into the stomach, more immediately impairs the digestive organs (444), causing morbid irritability, increasing the energy of the demand for stimulation, and leading to more ruinous effects on the animal, intellectual, and moral nature. Alcohol, a more rapidly diffusible and fiery stimulant (1539), whether in the form of distilled liquors or fermented, always acts on the body so as to impair its functions. It has been supposed to promote digestion ; but it is now certain that it always retards chymification (1378), and diminishes the power of the stomach. It cannot be used in any quantity without injury ; and when habitually used, does great mischief.

1553. Probably the most mischievous delusion is that which leads to the universal use of tea and coffee by old and young, rich and poor. The depraved appetite they create, the depression and demand for stimulation they cause, and the exhilaration they produce, make all with confidence believe that they are salutary cordials necessary to comfort. (1554.) ' Yet considering how early in life tea and coffee are introduced, and how universally they are used, it is greatly to be doubted whether they are not doing more injury than any other intoxicating substance. Besides the high temperature at which they are taken (1311), their strong narcotic property has the same effect as tobacco, opium, and alcohol (1531, 1552.)

1555. Narcotics diminish the size of the body, and otherwise impair its symmetry (963, 962). Employed as medicine, they often do great mischief. Even camphor and cologne are more frequently the sources of evil than good ;

and infusions of pungent herbs should be used with great caution, especially for children. Both in health and sickness, pure water is the most salutary liquid (1516.)

XXIV.

1560. Sleep is a repose of the organs, to afford the vital economy opportunity to repair exhaustion, waste, and injury from previous exercise or abuse (1419).

1567. The digestive organs should have little to do during sleep (1444) ; hence, it were better for every one to take no food nearer than three or four hours before retiring to rest (1440) ; also, every one, diseased or well, should avoid sleeping after a meal in the daytime ; for injurious effects sooner or later result from this habit. (1443.) Gentle exercise and amusement are better after a full meal than sluggish rest. (1501.)

1569. Men who have been most remarkable for longevity, have been long and sound sleepers.

1570. But it is not compatible with health to prolong rest beyond tolerably sound sleep ; continued drowsiness debilitates the system, and produces general langour. On the other hand, too little sleep causes excessive exhaustion of the vital energies (228.)

1572. Rocking children to sleep has a bad effect ; they will sleep as much as is good for them without ; and it is better they should occasionally cry and exercise their lungs, than be continually kept in sluggish quietness. No artificial means should be used to cause children to sleep.

1573. Old people require less sleep than the young or middle-aged. (1496.) But it is important that their sleep should be as sound as it can be rendered by *natural and proper means* (1567).

1574. Those who get a considerable portion of sleep before midnight are the most healthy and long-lived. As a general rule, the *latest hour* at which any one should be kept from sleep is ten at night. Six hours is the shortest time man can sleep, consistently with his permanent welfare ; and perhaps eight hours are as many as any one can enjoy to advantage.

1575. Feather-beds possess not one redeeming quality to save them from the bonfire to which they ought to be consigned.

1577. They render the skin more susceptible to cold (490), and debilitate the whole system (299.) They ought to be discarded by every human being.

1578. Feathers being non-conductors, retain so much of the perspired substances as to keep the body surrounded by a very impure atmosphere. Besides, there is more or less of decayed animal matter belonging to the feathers, continually undergoing decomposition, and forming unwholesome gases.

1579. Mattresses made of hair are more favourable to health than feather-beds. Moss, manilla grass, husks, straw, hay, palm-leaf, &c., are still more conducive to the well being of the body. Bodily symmetry (937), vigour, and activity are best promoted by a hard bed.

1580. It is important that the bedclothes should be properly regulated. Too many bedclothes debilitate the body, while the want of sufficient clothing impairs the soundness of sleep.

1581. Woollen blankets are the best clothing for beds ; for while sufficiently

H

non-conducting to retain the heat, they are not utterly impervious to the air and the exhalations of the body.

1583. In the morning, the bedclothes should be thrown over chairs, the bed shaken up, and the windows opened, so that the whole may be thoroughly aired before the bed is made.

1585. They who neglect air and cleanliness cannot expect to enjoy health, nor need they be surprised if they are visited with typhus and other fevers.

1586. Bedrooms should be large and well ventilated. Open chambers merely clapboarded on the outside, and not ceiled or plastered inside, are far more healthy bedrooms than those closely plastered. Both sleeping and awake, pure air cannot have too free access, provided we are sufficiently warm. (1580.) A screen should be placed before open bedroom windows, so that the sleeper is never exposed to a current. Where bedrooms open into a hall, it is perhaps better to open the windows of the hall and the bedroom door, than the windows of the sleeping-room There should be a fire-place, for ventilation, but not for fire, except during sickness ; for to sleep in a room where a fire is kept during the day is exceedingly unfavourable to health, unless the room be well ventilated before and during the night.

1589. Daily bathing should never be neglected.

1590. Every house should be constructed with convenience for bathing. Where such cannot be had, a portable bath may be placed in every sleeping-room ; or a pail of water, with a sponge, will answer the purpose.

1591. On rising, water should be applied freely to the face and neck ; and if the hair is short, the whole head may be plunged in. If there be a tub to stand in, take a tumbler and pour water upon the shoulders, and wash briskly in every part. This is a luxury. If nothing to stand in, take a sponge or towel, as wet as it can be without dripping, and pass briskly over the whole body ; wring it out, rub again vigorously, and wipe dry with a coarse towel. This should be followed with a flesh-brush, as stiff as the skin can bear, to the spine, limbs, &c., or use the hand alone.

[*To sit in a hip bath containing two or three inches of water, and squeeze a large sponge over the head and back, may be a more convenient method.*]

1592. By such operations as these, the skin is cleansed and invigorated, and the whole system healthfully exercised. The dyspeptic should exercise the abdomen (175) with the hands or handle of the flesh-brush, and passing it quickly up and down many times.

1594. The cold shower bath [received on the back, chest, and shoulders, the head being turned aside], is invigorating to those able to bear it, and beneficial to most dyspeptics labouring under chronic debility ; in some cases it is useful to repeat this bath before going to bed.

1595. The tepid bath, varying from eighty to ninety-five degrees, Fah., may be employed with advantage by all classes. The robust, when exhausted with toil, will find this bath exceedingly refreshing. The feeble, labouring under chronic diseases, are also benefited by the tepid bath, and the frequent use of it by aged people is highly salutary. No one should bathe soon after eating ; three hours at least should elapse after a meal, before a bath is taken.

1596. The vapour bath, as a remedial means, when properly employed, is highly salutary.

1597. Swimming is a healthy mode of bathing combined with exercise, for the vigorous. But boys are apt to remain in the water too long, and thereby often bring on disease. Those who cannot swim ought not to remain in over five minutes, and those who swim should not exceed thirty minutes. After any kind of bath, exercise is beneficial.

1598. The tepid bath is of service in diarrhœa, dysentery, &c., and persons may be astonishingly benefited by the tepid sponge bath, in certain stages of fever, when the pulse is full and quick, the tongue dry, the thirst great, and the skin hot, without a sense of chilliness. Effects almost miraculous are produced by sponging the body in such conditions, with tepid water containing a little soap or pearlash ; but judgment is necessary to govern such operations with safety.

1599. In the use of the cold bath, if, after rubbing and clothing, the individual is disagreeably chilly, unless conscious of having been in the water too long, he should avoid that kind of bathing, and perhaps confine himself to the tepid bath two or three times a week, or to the sponge bath, if he finds it refreshing to him.

1602. When baldness is threatened, the only remedy is to pay strict attention to diet and regimen ; cut the hair often short, wash the head in cold water, and follow the bathing with the brisk application of a stiff brush. If this does not restore the hair nothing will. All kinds of oil and perfumery should be avoided.

1603. It is of the utmost importance that the lungs be constantly supplied with pure air for the health of the blood and the welfare of the system. Crowded assemblies rapidly consume the oxygen of the air, and produce carbonic acid gas ; consequently, if not well ventilated, the air will soon become impure. In this manner the lives of many have been destroyed ; but a vastly greater number has been cut off by plagues, putrid, typhus, and other fevers, brought on or excessively aggravated by impure air. And it is principally owing to want of proper ventilation that cities are less healthy than the country.

1614. The materials used for clothing should be such as least to debilitate the skin, and so adjusted as to admit air to the body, and of free circulation, respiration, &c.

1615. Stays, garters, and every kind of compression should be avoided. The growing body should be as free as air.

1616. Much has been said in favour of wearing flannel next the skin ; and the habit being formed, had better be continued, than too suddenly abandoned. Yet woollen serves to excite and debilitate the skin, and thereby to increase the evils it is worn to prevent (1581.) Therefore, it is better not to wear woollen next to the skin.

1617. Fire relaxes and debilitates the system, and diminishes the power of the body to regulate its own temperature (130, 490) ; therefore, we should only use fire as a necessary evil. Our rooms should be so warmed as to be of mild and equal temperature in every part.

1619. Exercise promotes circulation (475) and respiration. It is the most important natural *tonic* of the body, and serves to impart vigour and energy to the mind.

1622. A certain amount of exercise or labour is as essential to the welfare of man, as food or air.

1623. If man takes too little exercise, he suffers ; and if exercise be excessive, he suffers.

1624. Natural labour is the cultivation of the soil ; and four hours a day each is about the amount the highest good requires.

1625. Society requires that many should be devoted to pursuits which do not admit of sufficient exercise for health.   But in order to be most beneficial, exercise must be enjoyed, losing the idea of labour in that of pleasure. Walking is doubly salutary when it can be connected with cheerfulness, and varied with running, leaping, &c.   Riding on horseback, the most efficient kind of exercise for invalids, is far more beneficial when the idea of riding for health is lost in some pleasing interest.

1626. The influence of music, connected with exercise, is very great ; hence, dancing is one of the most salutary of enjoyments (1627). Vocal music ought to be as universal a branch of education as reading, and instrumental music should be extensively cultivated.   Every evening the whole domestic circle—parents, grand-parents, children and grand-children—should have an opportunity to join in the dance.

1629. Action is as natural to children as breathing, and it is cruel to repress their instinctive desire beyond what is necessary.   Girls should be allowed as much freedom of action as boys, and they should be encouraged to exercise freely in the open air.

1630. Aged people must keep up their exercise ; and exercise of the mind serves also to prolong life.

1631. Dyspeptic and other chronic invalids ought never to hope for health without exercise.   The beneficial effects of horseback-riding in consumption are astonishing.   Invalids too feeble to mount, by riding a short distance the first time, and increasing the length daily, have become able, in the course of two weeks, to ride twenty miles without stopping, and to feel more vigorous at the end.

1632. The regular action of the bowels is of the utmost importance to health. The evils resulting from habitual costiveness are incalculable ; yet this habit of body is exceedingly common.   Mothers, and all who have the care of children, ought to pay great attention to this matter ; for it cannot be neglected without much hazard to life. [*When costiveness exists, much pain may sometimes be prevented by supporting the surrounding muscles with the fingers.*]   Costiveness predisposes to almost every form of disease ; and when it does not develop disease in youth, it lays a deep foundation for it in after life.   Habits should be so regulated as to secure free action of the bowels once every day.

INDEX.

(Compiled for the edition of the complete work published by the late Mr. George Dornbusch, here printed entire. The original edition had no index.)

N.B.—THE NUMBERS REFER TO THE PARAGRAPHS.

VOCABULARY, OR DEFINITIONS.

Abnormal—irregular, deformed, out of the truly natural state, condition, order, or manner.

Acute disease—disease which comes on suddenly, with violent symptoms, and soon comes to a crisis.

Alimentary canal—the stomach and intestines; the cavity which receives and digests the food, 317.

Albuminous—partaking of albumen, or a substance like the white of an egg.

Anastomosis—properly the communication of one vessel with another; when applied to other tissues it means to unite, to join, to run one into another.

Anus—mouth of the rectum through which the fæces are discharged.

Aorta—the great arterial or principal bloodvessel leading from the heart, 374.

Aperient—opening, laxative.

Asphyxia—a suspension of the action of the heart and arteries, as in swooning, fainting.

Atony—relaxation, debility, want of tone, 1180, Note.

Auricle (a little ear)—Applied to the two upper cavities of the heart, which resemble an ear, 363.

Bronchia—the branches of the windpipe in the lungs.

Cachectic—a vitiated state of the solids and fluids; a general want of health and tone.

Calculi (plural of calculus)—concretions, stone-like substances formed in the bladder, kidneys, gall-bladder, etc.

Caliber—the diameter of a body, the capacity of a tube.

Caloric—producing heat, 489.

Capillary—very small, hair-sized.

Cerebrum—the brain, 265.

Cerebellum—the little brain, 264.

Cerebro-spinal—the brain and spinal marrow taken together, 229.

Cervicle—belonging to the neck, 180.

Chronic Disease—disease of long standing, which comes on by imperceptible degrees.

Chyle—the fluid formed from the chyme, and from which the blood is formed, 153, 456.

Chylopoetic—having the power to form chyle.

Chyme—the digested food in the alimentary cavity, 435.

Cineritious—having the colour of ashes.

Cæcum—a portion of large intestine, 346.

Colon—the main portion of the large intestine, 338, 346.

Congestion—an accumulation of blood in a part, an over fulness of the vessels.

Corpora quadrigemina—four small ganglions lying at the top of the medulla oblongata, 250.

Corpus callosum—the great commissure of the brain, 267, 271.

Corpuscle—an extremely small body, a minute particle.

Crassamentum—the clot, or thick red part of the blood which separates from the serum, 482.

Cribriform—resembling a sieve or riddle, perforated with holes.

Cutis vera—the true skin.

Diaphragm—the membranous partition which divides the body into two large cavities, 175, 363.

Diabetes—disease of the kidneys, producing an excessive quantity of urine.

Depuration—cleansing, purifying.

Duodenum—the first twelve inches of the small intestines, 396.

Emphysematous—inflated, blown up, distended with air.

Encephalic—within the skull, the contents of the cranium.

Epigastric—round about the stomach.

Epiglottis—the little valve that closes the top of the windpipe in the act of swallowing, 340.

Et. Seq.—(et sequitur), and the following.

Facial—pertaining to the face.

Fascicle—a little bundle.

Fauces—the throat, the cavity behind the tongue.

Fribro-cartilage — cartilaginous structure with fibrous arrangement.

Filamentary—thread-like.

Final cause—purpose or end for which a thing is made or exists.

Follicle—a little glandular sac, 332.

Foramen—a hole, an opening.

Function—the office of an organ: thus, digestion is the function of the stomach.

Functional—pertaining to function.

Functional result—the effect of function: thus, chyme is the functional result of digestion.

Ganglion—a knot, bulbous enlargement of the nervous substance.

Gastric—belonging to the stomach.

Glosso-pharangeal—belonging to the tongue and pharynx.

Glottis—the opening or mouth at the top of the windpipe, 354.

Hepatic—belonging to the liver.

Humoral pathology—disease as connected with the humours or fluids of the body.

Hypoglossal—under the tongue.

Idiopathic disease—an original disease of some particular part, one that is not sympathetic, does not spring from another.

Idiosyncrasy—a peculiar temperament or predisposition.

Ileo cæcal—pertaining to the ileum and cæcum, 346.

Ingesta—the contents of the stomach after a meal is made.

Inorganic—not being arranged into organs, or by organs; stones and all substances not vegetable nor animal are inorganic.

Inosculate—to unite, the mouth of one vessel opening into another.

Jejunum—the second portion of the small intestine, so called because mostly found empty, 388.

Lacteals—small vessels that form the chyle and convey it to the thoracic duct, 387.

Lamina—plates of sheets.

Larynx—the top of the windpipe, 353, 354.

Lymphatics—small vessels that form the lymph and convey it to the bloodvessels, 385.

Medulla oblongata—the head of the spinal marrow, 244.

Menstruum—a dissolvent, a fluid holding other substances in a liquid state, 482.

Meso-colon—the membrane which as a curtain holds the colon in its place, 350.

Mesentery—the curtain of the small intestine, 350.

Molecular—pertaining to molecules or minute atoms.

Morbid—diseased, unhealthy.

Mucous membrane—the membrane which lines the stomach, lungs, etc., 339.

Nasal fossæ—the canals of the nose.

Normal—truly natural and proper state, form, condition, action.

Œsophagus—the meat-pipe, 338.

Olivary bodies—portions of the medulla oblongata, 244.

Omenta—the caul or the fatty curtains that cover the bowels, 350.

Ophthalmic—pertaining to the eye.

Organic—having organs, or being organised; any vegetable or animal body, or any solid substance belonging to such bodies.

Osseous—bony. Ossification—formation of bone.

Papulæ—the little velvety tufts or eminences formed by the fine terminations of nerves and vessels, 287.

Pancreas—a gland lying behind the stomach, 342.

Pathology—the science of disease, everything pertaining to disease.

Pelvis—the basin formed by the hip bones and others at the lower part of the trunk.

Pericardium—the membranous sac that surrounds the heart, 363.

Periostium—the fibrous membrane that surrounds the bones, 169.

Peristaltic—the worm-like motion of the intestines, 445.

Peritoneum—the outer coat of the stomach and intestines, 350.

Pharynx—the funnel-shaped muscular bag at the top of the meat-pipe, 338, 347.

Phrenitis—delirium or frenzy from inflammation of the brain, eta.

Physiology—the science of life, comprehending all the vital properties, powers, functions, and laws of living bodies.

Physiological depression—a state of exhaustion and relaxation, and want of tone or energy, 1180.

Physiologico-psychological science—intellectual and moral physiology; or the science of man's intellectual and moral nature as connected with the organs and functions of the living body.

Pleura—the membrane that lines the chest, etc., 361.

Plexus—a net-work of nerves or vessels.

Pneumo-gastric—pertaining to the lungs and stomach.

Preternatural—more than is natural or consistent with sound health.

Prophylactic—preserving health, conducive to health.

Psychology—the doctrine of the soul, including all the properties, powers, functions and laws of the intellectual and moral nature of man.

Puerperal—pertaining to child-bearing.

Pulmonary—belonging to the lungs.

Pylorus—the muscular ring at the lower orifice of the stomach.

Ramuscles—minute branches.

Rectum—the lower part of the large intestine, 338.

Renal—pertaining to the kidneys.

Rugæ—the wrinkes or small folds of the stomach, 349.

Saponaceous—having the quality of soap.

Scirrhus—indurated, hard, knotty.

Sebacious follicles—producing an oily or fatty substance.

Secernent—secreting, as follicles and glands, 333.

Semilunar ganglion—the central brain of organic life, 226.

Serous fibrous—partaking of the character of the serous and fibrous structure.

Serous—thin, watery ; like whey.

Serous membrane—the membrane which lines the closed cavities, and exhales a thin watery fluid or vapour, 176, 353.

Serum—the watery part of the blood, 482.

Solar plexus—the great central nervous plexus of the body, 226.

Stamina—the fundamental powers of the constitution.

Tissue, cellular, muscular and nervous—the three general forms of structure in the body, 312.

Tissue—a particular arrangement of fibres or filaments in an organ.

Therapeutics—the discovery and application of remedies in curing disease.

Trachea—the windpipe.

Trifacial nerve—the nerve of sensation, etc., with three branches distributed to the face, etc., 254, et seq.

Trisplanchnic nerve—see 226.

Turgescence—swollen, enlarged.

Vascular—consisting of vessels, see 313.

Vasculo-nervous—consisting of vessels and nerves, 267.

Vena-cava—the great venous trunk, see 378.

Vena-porta—a particular apparatus of veins connecting the alimentary canal and liver, see 381.

Venous blood—the dark purple blood of the veins.

Villi—the velvety pile of the mucous membrane, 327.

Viscera—the internal organs, see 313.

Vulnerary—adapted to heal wounds.

JOHN HEYWOOD, Excelsior Printing and Stationery Works, Hulme Hall Road, Manchester.

THE VEGETARIAN SOCIETY.

ESTABLISHED A.D. 1847.

President—Professor F. *I*. Newman, Weston-super-Mare.

Vice-Presidents.

T. Baker, Esq., Barrister, Wokingham.	Rev. W. N. Molesworth, M.A., Rochdale.
Edwin Collier, Esq., Manchester.	Isaac Pitman, Esq., Bath.
Rev. C. H. Collyns, M.A., Wirksworth.	John Storie, Esq., J.P., Prestonkirk, N.B.
Colonel J. M. Earle, London.	Graf Von Viettinghoff, M.D., London.
William Hoyle, Esq., Tottington, Bury.	Rev. F. Wagstaff, Great Barr, Birmingham.
Edward Hare, Esq., C.S.I., Bath.	W. Gibson Ward, Esq., Ross.
Mrs. Algernon Kingsford, Shrewsbury.	Howard Williams, Esq., M.A., Lytham.

Treasurer, John Davie, Esq., Dunfermline.—*Honorary Secretaries*, Rev. Jas. Clark, 1, Albion Place, Crescent, Salford ; and Mr. T. H. Barker, Cecil Street, Greenheys, Manchester.—*Secretary*, Mr. R. Bailey Walker, 91, Oxford Street, Manchester.

OBJECT.—To induce habits of abstinence from the Flesh of Animals as Food.

CONSTITUTION. —The Society is constituted of a President, Vice-President, Treasurer, an Executive Committee, a Secretary, and an unlimited number of Members and Associates above the age of fourteen years, who have subscribed to the Declaration of the Society. The Forms of Declaration can be obtained on application to the Secretary.

DEFINITIONS.—(*a*) A " Member " agrees to *adopt* the Vegetarian system of Diet, pays a yearly subscription, may *vote* at the Society's meetings, receive the Society's magazine, and is eligible for election to any office of the Society.—(*b*) An " Associate " agrees to *promote* the Vegetarian system, pays a yearly subscription, may *attend* the Society's meetings, and receive the Society's magazine.—(*c*) A " Subscriber " pays a yearly subscription, and receives the Society's magazine.

SUBSCRIPTIONS.—The Society is supported by (1) Members, (2) Associates, and (3) Subscribers, to each of whom the Society's magazine is posted monthly. Supporters of each class contribute a minimum subscription of half-a-crown a year.

Post-office Orders should be made on Manchester ; Cheques and Orders to be payable to R. Bailey Walker.

The following, with other Publications, may be had by post from the Secretary,
91, Oxford Street, Manchester :—

Manifesto of the Vegetarian Society.—Twenty-four Reasons for a Vegetarian Diet.—Medical and Scientific Testimony in favour of a Vegetarian Diet.— How to Begin: or Hints for those commencing the Vegetarian practice.—**Address of the Vegetarian Society on Christian Missions.—Two Dietetic Experiences**, and other leaflets.—Price One Halfpenny each, or 1s. per hundred.

The Penny Vegetarian Cookery. Eighth Edition ; Revised.

Professor Newman's Article from " Frazer." Reprinted by permission. Price 1d.

The Scientific Basis of Vegetarianism. By R. T. TRALL, M.D. Price 1d.

The Vegetist's Dietary and Manual of Vegetable Cookery. Compiled in accordance with the teachings of SYLVESTER GRAHAM, and published for the Vegetarian Society of England. Price 6d.; cloth, 1s.

The Dietetic Reformer, price Twopence monthly ; sent post free for one year, to any address, for Half-a-crown ; specimen copy for Two Stamps.

⁎ **The Society's " Manifesto," " Twenty-four Reasons," " How to Begin,"** and fuller List of Publications. posted free to any inquirer whose name may be communicated to the Secretary. ———

DEPOT: 91, OXFORD STREET, MANCHESTER.

Lightning Source UK Ltd.
Milton Keynes UK
UKHW020646070223
416609UK00011B/2483